THIS LIMITED AND SIGNED FIRST EDITION

[signature]

HAS BEEN SPECIALLY BOUND
AND PRODUCED BY THE PUBLISHER

The Road to Happiness*

*IS ALWAYS UNDER CONSTRUCTION

LINDA GRAY

Regan Arts.

NEW YORK

Regan Arts.
65 Bleecker Street
New York, NY 10012

First Regan Arts hardcover edition, September 2015

Library of Congress Control Number: 2015930625

ISBN 978-1-941393-09-3

Interior design by Nancy Singer
Jacket and Cover design by Richard Ljoenes
Jacket art © Robert Erdmann

Printed in the United States of America

10 9 8 7 6 5 4 3 2 1

This book is dedicated to my family:
Jeff Thrasher, Kehly, Lance, Ryder, and Jack Sloane.

I am so proud to be your mother and grandmother.

A special thanks to Lily Tomlin, who said,
"The road to success is always under construction."

CONTENTS

The Road to Happiness*

*IS ALWAYS UNDER CONSTRUCTION

HELLO

Next week I will turn seventy-five years old. My road to happiness has been long, but, as I enter this wonderful phase of my life I believe that the coming years will be among the best ones yet, filled with insight, creativity, and confidence. I have not only accepted that life continues on (hurling surprises at me every so often), I have surrendered to its unpredictability and learned to navigate the potholes, detours, and traffic jams.

I know my strengths and my weaknesses and I'm OK with all of them. The fear, guilt, and resentments I felt when I was younger have receded. The worry, judgment, criticism, and bitterness I experienced years ago have given way to forgiveness, peace, lightheartedness, and playfulness. I'm older, I'm wiser, and I'm more fun. I can laugh and I can play and I can bounce back.

When I break down or am run off the road, I get back up and put one foot in front of the other. That's a choice I make. That's a choice that you can make. You can keep moving or lie there and dwell on your troubles and become cranky and crotchety. You can choose to be grumpy or curious. You can choose to learn something new: study a foreign language or try a new food. Change your mind about something. Try a new hobby; start a new project. Explore.

Do you feel old and useless, that it's too late for you? Do you feel hopeless and stuck, thinking, "What's the use of trying something new? I'm too old." Life is a gift to be nourished and these negative attitudes will, with time, wither you and turn your life to stone. But, the choice is yours. The choice between life and death, joy and fear, energy and exhaustion. Each is as simple and profound a choice to make as turning left or right on the road of life. Choose wisely.

Recently, I gave my son a fiftieth birthday party. After half a century, all I remember about our first meeting was how my heart opened, how much love I felt for him in an instant. I remember telling my husband Ed in the delivery room, "I feel like we're the only three people in the world right now." His fiftieth served as proof of just how fast time goes, and as a reminder that we must honor each day's passing with love, to give all we can to create a planet where all babies are born into a nurturing, safe environment. It can be done. One person's love can spread around the world. It's vital, especially at this age, to love with an open heart, give all you can, and honor each day as the blessing it is. Now is not the time to turn back or pull over. It's our obligation as citizens of the planet to share our wisdom, experience, and creativity.

My life has been a full one. I have learned many things. I have loved and been loved. I value both the giving and receiving. My goal for this book is to share stories about my life, about the giving and receiving, and the things I've learned. Some of the life lessons were hard, but each made me wiser and less afraid. I expect the lessons to keep on coming. The road to happiness, and wisdom, is always under construction. Being unafraid and authentic have been my life's work. I think it shows. I look pretty good, not "for my age." For *any* age. My smile, the light in my eyes, and a positive attitude are the results of a life well lived, fears banished, grudges forgotten, and conflicts resolved. As I look back, I see that life has unfolded with divine timing—and not without many speed bumps along the way. There are three words I'd like to focus on: Time, Love, and Give. They are my compass. They define who I am and where I'm going.

Sharing my stories and ideas is the gift I'm giving to myself, and to you, to celebrate my seventy-fifth birthday. For volume two, you'll have to wait another seventy-five years.

HOW TO SHAPE
INTO SOMETHING IN
75 YEARS OR LESS

A few years ago, Jeffrey Lane, my longtime publicist called to tell me that *People* magazine asked to photograph me for their annual "Sexiest People Alive" issue.

"I think they have me confused with someone else," I said.

"No, they want you. Well, not you. They want your legs," replied Jeffrey.

Well, shucks. What seventy-two-year-old wouldn't be pleased to hear that? At my age, to be included in the issue with all those young, hot things was an unexpected, unbelievable honor. I had my doubts that it was for real until I arrived at the shoot with photographer Robert Erdmann.

He draped me in faux fur, sat me on a chair, and said, "Let's see those gorgeous gams of yours!"

A young woman from the magazine interviewed me. I told the story of a long-ago modeling gig. In 1966 a photographer called and asked, "Can you come in for an hour? We need legs." I went to the studio. He had me sit on the edge of a chair and roll on silk stockings while he took pictures of my legs. A few months later, my gams became iconic in the movie poster for *The Graduate*. Everyone assumed they were Anne Bancroft's. She must have been out of town or she wasn't consulted at all about the poster. The movie producers probably said, "Let's do a poster—*with legs!*" and they called me. Dustin Hoffman was cut and pasted in later. I got $25. Easy money.

The photo and article ran and I ran with it, doing a round of publicity. Naturally, every headline went something like this:

"Linda Gray, **72**, Bares Legs—and They're Not Hideous!"

Everyone seemed shocked that my limbs were not withered and deformed by varicose veins, liver spots, sagging skin, and wrinkles. It was fabulous to be included in the magazine and I adored the photo (so much so, you'll see it on the cover of this book). But enough with the astonishment that a woman my age has still got the goods. As Diana Vreeland once said, "I loathe narcissism, but I approve of vanity." I've got it. I flaunted it. I'd do it again.

Of all my body parts, my legs have been a particular source of pride—and income. As a model, my legs put food on the table and paid my rent. If not for my stems, Elizabeth Taylor wouldn't have given me the charming epithet "the bitch with the long legs." Unlike my eyes—my other distinctive part—I have never taken my legs for granted. Since age five, I've lavished them with care and thanked God for their enduring service. They're a blessing, one you can't fully appreciate unless you lose them.

• • •

When I was born in 1940, our president was Franklin Delano Roosevelt. Like our nation's fearless leader, my paternal grandfather, Leslie Vincent Gray, had been paralyzed by polio. Before then he'd been vigorous and athletic. At sixteen, he lied about his age to work on the railroad, shoveling coal into train engines. He was in his late teens when flu-like symptoms drove him into bed. He never walked again.

As a young girl, I thought Grandpa's wheelchair was the coolest. My baby sister, Betty, and I would climb on his lap and he would ferry us around Culver City, the Southern California suburb where we lived. I remember people waving at us, the gentle jostling of the wheels on the sidewalk, his strong chest and arms, the smell of Old Spice and pipe tobacco. I was the luckiest kid in the world.

Despite his being confined to a wheelchair, nothing slowed Grandpa down. He married (twice) and fathered three sons. A visionary and an inspiration to others with physical disabilities, he invented poles that attached to the gas and brake pedals so that paralyzed people could drive a car using just their hands. When Betty and I got too big to ride on his lap, Grandpa invented a go-cart attachment for his wheelchair so we (and my cousins and a few dogs), could ride along. We called it Grandpa's Widget. He was so full of life, I never thought of him as disabled or impaired. One of our grandpas walked and one wheeled around. That was just how it was.

Grandpa Gray was a jeweler. He, my dad, and my Uncle John ran Gray's Jewelers in Culver City. One of Dad's claims to fame was that he made Clark Gable's watch fob for *Gone With the Wind*. The "Gray Boys" got more work from MGM and made a name for themselves on the periphery of showbiz.

After school at St. Augustine's, we would walk across the street to MGM and sit on the curb in our blue-and-white uniforms with our little autograph books and wait for movie stars to drive in or to leave the studio lot. Our exciting after-school activity! The cars—Packards, Lincolns—were unique and special just like the stars themselves. Van Johnson, Carmen Miranda, and Stewart Granger all seemed bigger than life. They all stopped and graciously signed autographs for us.

Mom had an artistic background, too. She was an illustrator, designer, and ballerina. They met through mutual friends in the art world. After a very short engagement, they married at St. Augustine's Church, across the street from the MGM studio, in 1939. (I would take my own vows there in 1962.) Soon after her wedding, Mom got pregnant with me and stopped working. My sister came four years later. If Mom were a young woman now, I don't think she would have given up her career to be a stay-at-home mom. I don't believe she really wanted to be a mom, but in those days, that was what women did. After I was born, her only creative outlet was decorating the Gray Jewelers storefront windows. She arranged the drapery and jewelry beautifully, and people would stop on the street to look and admire her creativity.

I was five in 1945, the same year FDR died. I came down with a bad sore throat and was sent to bed. The next day, I couldn't move my legs. My parents suspected the worst and rushed me to the hospital. Their fears were confirmed by the young doctor in the ER. I'd contracted polio. The virus had infected the cells of my central nervous system that linked my brain and my muscles. My legs were no longer connected to my brain. I could think, *Run! Play! Dance!*, but my body didn't respond. I would touch the skin of my legs and feel the sensation of pressure and sometimes pain. But when I tried to move them, nothing happened.

It was weird, but I wasn't nearly as upset as my parents. Both fell into a depression about my diagnosis. Even at five, I remember Mom holding onto a glass. Having a dangerously sick child when she was barely older than a kid herself, with not a lot of emotional support form my stoic father, plus a new baby at home? Mom had a very hard time. She went from being a social drinker to an alcoholic and for years I harbored a secret guilt that it was my fault.

Grandpa didn't seem to mind spending his life in a wheelchair. So how bad could it be? I imagined the two of us wheeling around the neighborhood, him in his big chair and me in a little one, waiving at his friends, the dogs running alongside. I told my mother how fun it would be and she burst into tears.

Mom and Dad were terrified of the unknown. For some kids, their body's immune system knocked out the polio virus before damage was permanent. For others, the virus burned through nerve cells at an un-stoppable rate, affecting limbs and lungs. Thousands of polio kids from the 1940s and '50s were put into iron lungs, 800-pound airtight metal ventilators, to breathe for them.

My doctors recommended to my parents that even though my lungs were as yet unaffected by the virus, they should put me in the metal canister anyway. Back then it was standard treatment. Newspa-pers and magazines ran photos of hundreds of polio kids in row upon row of iron lungs. They looked like giant batteries with human heads. The treatment did save lives, but it wouldn't have been appropriate for my case. If I'd been put in one, it could have weakened my lungs and limbs, and possibly resulted in my having a lifetime of pulmonary problems like asthma or put me in a wheelchair for life.

My parents went with the alternative "Raggedy Ann" treatments instead. Mom would stand at the foot of my bed, lift up one of my legs, and then let it drop back down again. We did this exercise daily for months. It was the highlight of my day. Otherwise, I was quarantined in my bedroom. Although polio isn't contagious, people were petrified of it. My friends came to my window to wave at me and talk through the glass. I spent a lot of time drawing flowers on embossed paper nap-kins that Mom would then distribute to my pals.

Over a period of several months, my legs slowly regained func-tion. My doctors kept a close eye on me and eventually declared me "cured." Part of me was disappointed I wouldn't get to cruise around the neighborhood with Grandpa, but I could go run around with my friends. It felt great to get outside after months in bed.

As soon as I could walk, my parents set about strengthening my legs and signed me up for dance class. Mom sewed a beautiful costume for my first recital, a red velvet leotard and tutu with white marabou feathers. I was so excited to wear it. Everyone I knew was in the audience. They all came to see the polio baby—snatched out of the claws of paralysis—dance.

Another kid, Freddie Phillips (how in the world did I remember his name?) was going to play the piano while I did my number. The song was called "Little Girl," and was a real humdinger. I waited in the wings for the first notes and then dashed onto the stage on healthy legs to wild applause. I was so excited to be the center of attention that I just stood there, paralyzed. I completely forgot the steps. It was scarier than my limp months as a Raggedy Ann doll. Freddie continued playing the piano, slower and louder. After what seemed like an eternity, something clicked and I started my routine. Later on, Mom said she didn't notice my gaff. From her perspective, my walking onto the stage at all was a miracle.

Walking is still a miracle. I'm grateful for my ability to do it. At my age—at any age—possessing two legs that function properly is a blessing. Possessing a pair of stems that are also considered the Sexiest Legs in the Entire Universe, circa 2012? I reveled in the honor and wasn't at all humble in accepting it.

Randomness imprinted in my mind at a young age. Why were some kids paralyzed for life and some cured? Was it fate, luck, divine intervention? Who knows? I have thought about this often and have accepted that we have so little control over what happens to us in our lives. But it is within our control to learn from our every experience. I never ask "Why me?" I ask "Why?" There is always a lesson, if you have the patience and will to figure it out.

I'm not paralyzed by fear about what might have been or what might be. I'm grateful for what is and I make excellent use of what I've got. I can put one foot in front of the other. I can traverse the world, be of service to myself and to people in foreign lands. The legs that once failed me have, seventy years later, been celebrated. I intend to keep them in good standing until both of my feet are in the grave.

WHAT SCARES YOU CAN ALSO HEAL YOU

The adults in my life were impressed that I overcame polio. But the kids in my school couldn't have cared less. At six, when I returned to class, I was just another girl—an awkward, ugly one at that. I had long, black, stringy hair and was stick thin. Everything about me was weak and awkward. My teeth, when they came in, were too big for my mouth, they grew out horizontally, like a horse.

Around age seven, a very delicate time of life when little comments can really destroy you, I was sitting in the auditorium at St. Augustine's for an assembly. I turned around, looking to find a friend. A row of boys sat directly behind me. As I turned, one said, "Whoa, look at those frog eyes!"

Along with the gross hair and buckteeth, I had enormous eyes. They're still quite large and I used them to communicate emotion when I became an actor. But during those early years, I looked like an alien from Planet Amphibian, and the boys in school didn't let me forget it for a minute.

I got braces, too, to complete the horror show of my adolescent look. I was deathly insecure and became paralytically shy. I couldn't make eye contact or speak to anyone other than my parents and sister. By the time I moved on to junior high at Notre Dame Academy, I kept my head down going from room to room to avoid talking to the other kids or the nuns. Needless to say, I didn't have many friends.

Life at home wasn't any easier for me. Mom's drinking escalated. It was a time when everyone had a wet bar with elaborate cocktail shakers with roosters etched on them, and glasses with the owners' initials in gold. Dad's habit was to have a couple of drinks when he got home from work. Mom hit the wet bar more often than he did. She spent more and more time in her haze, sewing and drawing, enlisting us in creative little projects, which, as a kid, were fun to do, but then we'd get hungry and realize she'd forgotten to shop for food.

I believe she wanted to be a good mother, but didn't know how. She wasn't a falling-down drunk; she just lived in her own blurry world. It was as if she'd given up on living in the world Betty and I were in. So I become a mother to Betty at a very young age. She was the mischievous one and I was the responsible one. I took care of her—got her dressed, gave her baths, did the laundry, shopped for food, and cooked dinner most every night. I got into cooking at age ten out of pure necessity. I would go to the corner market, which I walked to from our house, and get recipes from the butcher and other customers. I learned some of the Crock-Pot recipes I still make today.

On one of those shopping expeditions, Betty, only seven at the time, stole a bag of peanuts. I didn't realize until we were already home. I yelled at her for stealing and she was so worried she'd get in trouble, she disappeared. No one knew where she was. When nighttime came and Betty was still missing, my Dad and I searched the streets, enlisting all the neighbors in the hunt. We were just about to call the police when Betty came walking into the living room. She had been hiding in the back of her closet.

I sat down with Betty on the sofa and gave her a stern lecture about why she shouldn't ever do that again. I went on and on, really laying it on thick, and made Betty cry.

I became increasingly resentful about Mom as the years wore on. One night when I was fourteen, Betty and I confronted Dad while he was sitting at the dining room table, and we stood in front of him.

I said, "Dad, we want you to divorce Mom."

"What?"

"We don't like her and we think she should leave."

Betty and I begged him to get rid of her.

In hindsight, it was so cold-hearted. The woman was sick and needed help. But we were kids and all we wanted was a mom who smelled like fresh-baked cookies instead of Rose's lime juice and vodka. A classic high-functioning lady drinker, Mom got dressed (in pants; why couldn't she wear dresses like the other mothers), and could hold conversations. It wasn't like she passed out on the floor in her bathrobe. But there was always something that came between Mom and my sister and me, a substance that changed her voice, the way she looked at us, her smell, her energy. Most importantly, when she drank, she wasn't interested in caring for us. We would have preferred a mother who did.

Dad listened to us and then said, very quietly, "I love her."

His response was textbook codependence. He loved her and would rather keep her close and do nothing than force a change. His refusal to do anything was monumental for me. There would be no way out. I was truly trapped and under constant pressure.

In 1955, stress wasn't the well-known problem it is today, especially not in children. Today, parents get their kids into therapy or on Zoloft. But in those days, drugs and shrinks were for looneys. I was so shy, though, something had to be done or I'd be hiding in corners for the rest of my life.

A good friend of my parents, Cliff Bowman, was a facilitator at the Carnegie Training Center in Los Angeles. I liked Cliff. When he and his wife came to dinner at our home, he was nice to me and put me at ease. He came off as honest and powerful. In a word, *winning*. Cliff always had a worn copy of the classic 1936 book, *How to Win Friends and Influence People* with him. At one dinner when I was fifteen, I paged through it and we discussed some finer points. The lessons in the book seemed okay. Cliff convinced my parents that my going to one of his seminars would do me a world of good, and they signed me up.

I took the bus to class. Ten people, all older than me by at least a decade, sat in a circle. Cliff said, "Let's go around the room and introduce ourselves. Tell us your name and a little something about you."

The students were office managers, secretaries, just people who wanted to boost their careers or attract that special someone. I didn't register most of what they said about themselves, though, because mortification had made me deaf. When it was my turn to speak, I couldn't open my mouth.

It was agony to have a room full of strangers stare at me. I started to cry. Cliff skipped over me and went to the next person.

That night at home, Mom and Dad asked, "How'd it go?" I told them I wasn't able to speak. They said, "Okay, maybe next time."

The second week, I couldn't speak, either, but I was able to calm down and listen to what the others talked about. Cliff and the group went through Carnegie's 30 Principles, like the Ten Commandments, for success. I perked up about Principle #15: *Let the other person do a great deal of the talking.*

Clearly, I was born to win friends and influence people.

The third week, I was able to say my name, too softly. The group asked me to speak up, which freaked me out. Cliff asked, "Can you tell us something about yourself, Linda?"

Nope. I could not.

That night, the report to my parents was dire. Calling attention to my anxiety only made me more self-conscious about it. I couldn't hide at the group the way I did at school. "I hate it," I cried. "It's *torture.* Don't make me go back!" I begged them to let me quit. They were getting reports from Cliff, too, who was ever positive about my progress. They made me keep going.

The fourth week, I watched and listened to the other students talk through different scenarios using the Principles. One guy, Mack, was in real estate, so Cliff pretended to be his prospective buyer. Mack applied every Principle he could remember in his opener, such as Smile (#5), Begin in a Friendly Way (#13), Make the Other Person Feel Important—and Do It Sincerely (#9), Ask Questions (#25). He liberally used Remember That the Person's Name is to That Person the Sweetest Sound In Any Language (#6).

So his opener went something like this: "Howdy, Cliff. That's a sharp suit, Cliff. I can tell you're a very intelligent man, Cliff. So, tell me, Cliff, what do you like about this house? It's a beauty, all right. You've got great taste, Cliff!"

In hindsight, it reminds me of that Far Side cartoon, of the dog listening to his master talk. The thought bubble over the dog's head reads, "Blah, blah, blah, Ginger. Blah, blah, blah, Ginger."

By the tenth mention of Cliff's name, everyone in the class was cracking up, including me. When others took their turn, they added extra "Cliffs" to the end of their sentences and it became a running joke of the class. I drank it in, the camaraderie and laughter. Using the Principles was taking affect within the microcosm of the classroom. We were Good Listeners (#7) who Let the Other Person Save Face (#26), and Gave Honest and Sincere Appreciation (#2). As the silent observer, I could see how everyone's respectfulness added to the positive vibes in the room. There were no judgments here, only good intentions and the desire to do well.

I got comfortable in this idyllic society of normal (nonalcoholic or codependent) adults. I didn't feel judged or insecure. In my fifth class, to everyone's amazement, I raised my hand and asked to do a scene of my own. Cliff suggested I try a classic teenage-agony-column-worthy situation of sitting down at a cafeteria table with a group of girls.

I pretended to carry my tray to the table and sat down. I smiled so hard my cheeks hurt. And then, I spoke. The opening line of my official entry into human society:

"Hi, Amy! How's your Salisbury steak today, Amy? That's a cute dress, Amy! Wherever did you find it, Amy?"

It was a huge leap forward.

Between fifteen and eighteen, the braces came off. I grew into my eyes, got a decent haircut, and much to my amazement, became a teen model. At home, Mom kept drinking, but Betty was older and less dependent on me. Circumstances eased a bit. I applied the Carnegie Principles at school and they worked beautifully. By senior year at Notre Dame Academy, I was elected class president. I went from being the Girl Most Likely to Hide in a Corner to the Girl Most Likely to Arouse In Another Person an Eager Need or Want (#3).

As soon as I started talking—sincerely, with lots of questions and compliments, but also Being a Good Listener (#7)—I came out of my shell. Everything just seemed to flow as soon as I picked up that imaginary lunch tray of Salisbury steak.

I didn't connect the dots back then. But now I see it clearly. In that class, I tried acting for the first time. With Cliff and the gang, our aim was to dissolve conflict. In an improv class, you tried to escalate it. Opposite goals; similar strategies. In both cases, you used specific techniques to keep a conversation going and evoke emotion in others.

I came to associate acting with relief, calm, and confidence. I started doing plays at school. When I graduated high school, I was awarded with five stars as an upstanding member of the National Thespian Society, troupe number 525. That honor was almost as gratifying as my Emmy nomination twenty-five years later.

Although I had cursed my parents' names for making me stick with that Carnegie class, I'm so grateful that they did. My keenest childhood terror—speaking in public—turned out to be my occupation, my joy, and my passion. Acting has been, without a doubt, the enduring, great love of my life.

Dale Carnegie once wrote, "You can conquer almost any fear if you will only make up your mind to do so. For remember, fear does not exist anywhere except in the mind." You have to face your fears (may we all have people in our lives who help us do it) to break through to whatever marvels are on the other side. Fear adds years to your age. But breaking through them is like mainlining the wonder of a child.

I lived on a farm raising chickens for years (more on that very soon). My first hatching, I noticed one chick couldn't seem to break through its shell. So I helped him. I peeled away the pieces. I didn't know that the process of pecking through the shell was how baby chicks strengthened their tiny neck muscles so they could hold their heads up and feed. Because of my "help," the chick didn't survive.

I had to develop my social muscles to break through my shell and survive. For you, it might be something else. It's not easy to face what frightens you, but if you do, especially now, you'll be so much stronger for it. Good thing: We're at the age when we can flex our muscles and affect positive change in our personal lives and the world.

SUCCESSFUL WOMEN
DON'T GIVE UP

At sixteen, I was discovered by a photographer at a Mother's Day fashion show at Notre Dame Academy, an all-girls Catholic school. That led to modeling in a bathing suit on a beach for photography clubs. I struck a kittenish pose and a bunch of middle-aged men clustered around me, snapping my picture.

I moved on to catalog work, modeling skirt suits, hats, and gloves in jaunty poses that are laughably stiff by modern standards. One was the classic "I'm walking here!" and looked like the photographer yelled, "Freeze!" while I casually strolled across the seamless with a rictus grin. Other classic poses were "I'm standing here!" and "Is that the bus?" of pointing into the middle distance with hopeful eyes. At the time, white kid gloves and Madeline hats were cutting edge.

My next major job, at seventeen, was as a dress model in the Los Angeles showroom of Saul Rubenstein. Customers would come in and select a $3.99 dress off the rack. I'd change into it in a little room in the back and then emerge from behind a velvet curtain to trot around the store. I presented the dress in different dramatic poses, such as "gazing romantically out of the window" and "strolling with an imaginary poodle."

One day Saul said, "Linda, do you know why I hired you?"

"No, Saul. Why did you hire me?" Because I was a kid who worked for peanuts?

"Because you make those $3.99 dresses look like $39.99!"

I took it as a huge compliment. I loved Saul. He taught me about retail, how to wear a cheap dress like a ball gown, and how to order takeout at a Jewish deli. Before Saul, I'd never had a bagel with cream cheese and lox. I'll be eternally grateful to him for that alone.

At nineteen, a college sophomore, I faced a choice. Should I continue modeling for catalogs and calendars, and enjoy the travel and money that went with it, or should I put more effort into my classes, study hard, and become a doctor? (Not a common ambition for girls in 1959; it was unusual for girls to have *any* ambition to be anything beyond wife and mother.)

I needed a sign from the universe to point me in the right direction. And then a friend told me that *Glamour* was conducting a nationwide search for a "Glamour Girl." The winners of the contest would be featured in the magazine, wearing designer clothes (i.e., dresses that cost more than $3.99). Dazzled by the idea of becoming a high-fashion mannequin like Suzy Parker, I sent in my photos. I thought my face and hair were okay, going by what others told me. As you recall, I was Buckteeth Frog Eyes for most of my life until then and was still amazed that anyone thought I was pretty. I noticed that I'd changed, but it takes some time for the brain to catch up to the face. Plus, I didn't have a high-fashion body shape. Even as a teenager, I had a round behind. I remember one night my father was sitting on the couch when Mom, Betty, and I walked by him. He said, "It's like looking at three question marks." We all had the Gray Butt—round, bubbly, protruding. My daughter Kehly blames me for passing down the Gray Butt to her. At least for her, the question mark profile is in style. Back in the 1950s, a small, flat ass was in vogue—and I had (and still have) the opposite.

I thought it was a long shot, but I tried to stay hopeful. I waited to hear back from *Glamour*. And waited. And waited. Finally, the letter arrived a few days after Christmas, just a few months after my twentieth birthday.

December 27, 1960

Miss Linda Gray
4304 Mentone
Culver City, California

Dear Miss Gray,

Thank you very much for submitting your photograph to the Glamour girl search we are conducting.

I regret to say you are not the exact type of girl we are looking for. However we don't want you to be discouraged at this point. Perhaps if you changed your make up a little and tried some experimenting with new hair stylings, you too might very well shape into something. Good Luck.

Sincerely

Karlys Daly
Beauty Editor

KD/cr

And a very Happy New Year to you, Karlys Daly!

When faced with rejection, some women double down on pursuing their goals. For example, then recent college graduate Meryl Streep auditioned for the Jessica Lange part in *King Kong* in 1975. Producer Dino De Laurentiis called her "brutta" (ugly) to her face without realizing she spoke Italian. This did not deter young Meryl. She kept auditioning and a year later, landed a big part in *The Deer Hunter*. I doubt she's been rejected by anyone, for anything, since. Supreme Court Justice Sonia Sotomayer wrote in *My Beloved World* that as a freshman at Princeton, she got a C for an essay in English because she wasn't able to construct a coherent argument. Since then, she has shown signs of improvement.

Other women, when they hit a wall, find another door to walk through. Famous flexible flyers, off the top of my head: Mary Tyler Moore tried acting only because she couldn't get work as a dancer. Joni Mitchell gave songwriting and singing a shot when her painting career went nowhere. Diane von Furstenberg turned to fashion design because no one would hire her as a model.

Still other women are so wounded by rejection that they give up on their dreams. Sorry, no stories about famous women who took that route. Successful women don't give up. This anonymous quote puts it perfectly: "The secret to success is not to try to get rid of or shrink from your problems. The secret is to grow yourself so that you are bigger than your problems."

Ms. Daly's rejection defined the problem I would have to grow bigger than, that I had not yet "shape[d] into something." The beauty editor at *Glamour* thought I was an amorphous pasty ball of raw dough on the counter, with bad hair and makeup. What did she know? Clearly, her taste was not as refined as Saul Rubenstein's. Any girl could look good in a $500 frock. It took a special talent to pull off a $3.99 dress.

At the dawn of the *Mad Men* era, few women held executive power. I had no idea what kind of influence Ms. Daly wielded at the magazine, but she did possess the enormous power to crush teenage dreams. Part of what got under my skin about her rejection was that I didn't understand what shape I was supposed to take. My ideas about who I was and what I was going to become were blobby and undefined. But thanks to my lackluster makeup and offensive hair stylings, it was unlikely I'd shape into Veruschka.

If the letter had been a standard rejection along the lines of, "We regret to inform you [INSERT NAME HERE] that you are not a Glamour Girl. Better luck next year!" I would have balled it up, thrown it away, and gotten on with my identity crisis, already in progress. Her remarks were so personal, though, and my flaws so eloquently noted, I decided to keep the letter for future reference.

I don't know if Ms. Daly is still living. If she is, I'm sure she will now drop dead of shock to learn that I framed her letter and have displayed it prominently on my desk for the last fifty-five years.

At first, the letter was a motivational tool. I was determined to shape into something marvelous—whatever that was—and Karlys Daly was going to watch me do it. I'd show her. I'd show the *whole world*! It's possible that without the incentive of proving Ms. Daly wrong, I might've quit modeling, finished college, and would now be a retired cardiologist with an impressive golf handicap.

After a while, the letter became a trophy. I shaped into a TV star. My hair stylings won awards. My makeup tips and tricks were copied by girls all over the world and became the subject of countless articles in dozens of magazines (although, oddly, never *Glamour*). I became a cover girl at thirty-eight and wore designer frocks on the red carpet, at the White House, to shop for groceries.

Later still, the letter was a laugh. I'd look at it and crack up about how young and stupid I was then. I shaped into a mother and a grandmother, and watched the kids go through angst-ridden identity crises of their own. They moaned, "What am I going to do with my life?" I told them that they'd figure it out and that what seemed *devastating* at twenty would be a minor speed bump in the long and winding road of their lives. One day, they'd look back on the drama and laugh, just as I did. They didn't believe me, of course. They had to find out for themselves.

And now? The letter is a comfort. It's been around longer than my kids, my house, my career. I've taken so many shapes since I first received it. All of them fit together to tell the story of my life. My shape-shifting isn't nearly done, though. I continue to define and refine my sense of self. I'm still asking "What am I going to do with my life?" but with "oh, boy!" excitement, not "oh, God" anxiety.

No one can predict the shape of things to come. I don't want to know what's coming. I'm happy to wait to find out, which is another huge difference between twenty and seventy-five. As Elizabeth Taylor once said, "It's strange that the years teach us patience; that the shorter our time, the greater our capacity for waiting." When you get older, you know that life's mysteries are revealed in the fullness of time. All you have to do is wait, watch, and be amazed.

TOOT YOUR OWN HORN

Despite being a shapeless blob with ratty hair and clown makeup (and a round behind), I dropped out of college to model full-time. I still lived at home and continued to take care of Betty, guiding her through school and cooking for the family. I was fiercely loyal and protective of Betty, and was loath to leave her. But at twenty, the desire to get away from my family grew too strong to ignore. The only ways out were to make a lot of money or to get married.

I assumed I'd get married and have kids at some point. In those days, you had to get married to have sex and I was definitely interested in that. No one was banging down my door with roses and an engagement ring, so I went full force into modeling and landed gigs in bridal shows and swimwear catalogs. We were called "coat hangers." As a human hanger, I posed for catalogs and calendars, including one for Coke, holding a bottle of soda absurdly close to my face.

Calendars and catalogs were okay, but I'd never earn enough to get my own apartment doing them. In terms of money and prestige,

TV commercials would be a giant step up. Plus, they could lead to acting, which was my ultimate goal.

The faces selling deodorant and moisturizer in TV looked wholesome and approachable. I thought, *I can do that.* My agent wasn't as enthusiastic as I was. When I started asking her to send me on commercial auditions, she said, "But you're a model."

So? Surely, the commercial execs would be impressed by my poses. I wore my agent down and she sent me on a few auditions. The casting agents looked at my portfolio and said, "You can't do TV. You're a model. Models can't speak."

We were having a conversation. Clearly, I was capable of forming words and sentences with the subtle manipulations of my lips and tongue. "I am speaking to you right now," I said slowly, so they could understand.

It didn't matter. The prejudice against models as TV commercial actors was ingrained industry-wide. At every audition, they'd say, "You can't speak," while I proved them wrong by saying, "I'm talking here!" If they gave me a chance, I would gladly walk and talk *at the same time.*

I finally cajoled my way into one job, it lead to another, and eventually, by sheer dogged persistence, I became a regular on TV commercials, always playing a woman who was born, tragically, without vocal cords. I had many talents and skills. I could ride a horse on the beach, slather on face cream, and go canoeing in Hawaii. I could cook a delicious and nutritious meal for the whole family, repair a broken vase with miracle glue, wash my hair, lick a stamp, and buff hardwood flooring. I could roll on antiperspirant, which reminded me of body part modeling. *Okay, armpit! Get ready for your close-up!* Directors loved me for my all-American California girl look. But as a prototypical female, I was not permitted to speak.

Throughout that era, I sang the lament, "I am woman. *Let me roar!*" to every commercial casting director in Hollywood. None seemed to hear me.

When I was twenty-one, I got married to Ed Thrasher. It was expected of a newly married woman to put aside her career and devote herself to making a home and making babies, in that order. Modeling, it was assumed by nearly everyone, was the thing I did to attract a husband. So now that I had one, it was assumed that I would say good-bye to my work. I thought about it, certainly. I was out of my parents' house, so that prime motivator was gone. Ed made a good living as an art director. I didn't have to work for the money. For a short time after the honeymoon, I busied myself as a homemaker, decorating our apartment and cooking elaborate dinners for Ed like a good wife. I quickly came to realize that if I didn't have an outlet for my creativity, I might get bored and frustrated, and very possibly medicate myself at the wet bar just as my mother did. That idea alone was scary enough to keep my hand in the modeling world.

Also my pride would not allow me to quit. Getting to talk in commercials was an itch that I simply had to scratch. If I could land just one, then I could say, "I did it," and be done. I'd been told "no" so many times I couldn't stop trying until I got that one "yes." When someone said I couldn't do something, my feistiness was piqued and I just had to prove them wrong. Then I would gladly put down my makeup brushes and walk away. I was still doing non-talkies into my first pregnancy in 1964. In one, an ad for VO5 shampoo, I was eight months pregnant. I sat on a stool with a towel wrapped around me, and they shot it from the boobs up so no one could see my belly. So with a baby on board, I sat on that stool, lathered, rinsed, and repeated, then swung my hair around in ecstasy about how clean and shiny it was.

I loved being a new mom and decided to take a break. My last ad was for hair color and they dyed my hair red. During my son Jeff's infancy, I grew out the red, and had two-tone hair, and couldn't work even if I wanted to, which I didn't. Betty had a baby, too, named Leslie, a beautiful girl. As young new moms (she was eighteen when Leslie was born), we figured out how to care for our children together.

Then I had Kehly in 1966, and she had Mike. We were sisters who had survived, who escaped, and now we had a happy little tribe to love, enjoy, and nurture.

Of course when I'd stopped pushing to get a voice job, that's when the work started flowing. I was offered an ad for Vassarette bras, with a voiceover script. Here are my first recorded words as an actor, in the role of "Woman":

"Me? I'm practical. I like a classic car I can drive every day, ties my husband will really wear, and a bra that's comfortable, that makes whatever I wear look totally smooth. Like this one: the So Smooth bra by Vassarette. Look! No seams, which means no lumps or bumps."

I poured everything I had into that voiceover. This bra would protect the world from lumps and bumps. It would save marriages and stop rioting in the streets! Nipples be gone! I sold smoothness with everything I had, just to prove that the sound of my voice did not cause dogs to howl in the night.

Casting agents liked what they heard and I booked more commercials—and not just voiceovers with miming. Actual words came out of my actual mouth. Eventually I did over 400 TV ads, including a classic from *L'eggs* that might ring some bells.

Again, in the part of "Woman":

"Penny and I were feeding the elephant when she said, 'Mommy, the elephant has wrinkly pantyhose, just like yours.' It was terribly embarrassing! The little rascal was right. Now, I wear *L'eggs*. *L'eggs* have memory yarn. It stretches out and stretches back to fit beautifully!"

I had to be flexible to keep working. I came to appreciate that I had a life, a job, and a career. My life was my new family, obviously. My job was selling boxes and bottles by holding them really close to my face and smiling. My career, then and now, was to challenge myself, and keep pushing the limits of what others think I can do, and what I believe I'm capable of.

During my decade in advertising, I used a soft sell—gentle persistence and never giving up. I always knew where I wanted to go, even if I had no idea how to get there, or how long it would take, with many detours and road blocks.

To get what we want—a boyfriend, a friend, a job, respect, an invitation, a large donation for your charitable cause, an honest prognosis—you have to be an advocate for yourself. On the road to happiness, you have to toot your own horn. Don't depend on your husband, children, doctors, lawyers, bosses, accountants, agents, or anyone else. When you're doing your due diligence and challenging the wisdom of others, you'll feel energized by the effort. Vitality comes from taking charge, whether that means making a dinner reservation, pursuing a medical treatment, or writing your life story. No one cares about your interests as much as you do. I'm sorry, but it's true. If you care about seeing Tibet, or meeting your daughter's new boyfriend, or investing in green energy companies, make it happen. You are strong. You are invincible.

LOVE THE SKIN YOU'RE IN

Last year, I was in London in a production of *Cinderella* as the fairy godmother. My previous performance on the London stage was *The Graduate* in 2001. In the intervening fourteen years, my looks haven't changed all that much, which has made the British press very suspicious. Every interviewer has asked why I didn't look like death on heels. The answer had to be: (1) Botox, (2) a face-lift, or (3) a pact with the devil. Clean eating and living—aka, the truth—was not an acceptable reply.

One of the British tabloids ran an article with the headline:

"Actress Linda Gray, **74**, Shows Off Her Incredible Youthful Look."

One journalist said, "Your face moves," as if shocked.

I laughed and said, "So does yours."

On the way to work one day my cab driver told me he'd seen a big story on me online, filled with pictures. Of course, I looked it up—along with *Cinderella* stills—the article included a fourteen-photo array of my face over a forty-year span. In the captions, a plastic surgeon weighed in on the minute changes in my jaw line and counted every wrinkle.

Modern women are obsessed with aging. That article shook me up. It's not easy to put your face forward at any age. But then to see parts of it—my brow, my crow's feet, my neck—magnified to analyze every single sag, fold, and age spot? A teenager would shrink in horror under such scrutiny! It was mortifying. I thought high-definition television was humbling.

Despite the clear evidence that I do not possess the skin of a fifty-year-old, interviewers insisted that I must have gone under the knife. I was almost sorry to disappoint them.

I did one Internet interview with a sweet young woman who asked me to describe my beauty routine. I told her that I wash my face, use inexpensive moisturizer (never buy anything that costs $150 in a jar), and take a lot of walks in the fresh air. "Beauty comes from the inside," I said. She kept nodding, hoping for more. I felt bad about disappointing her, so I trotted out an old saying about makeup—"It's all about the eyes"—hoping it'd help. But I'm not a makeup artist. I sometimes experiment with makeup and hair stylings, as Karlys Daly, *Glamour* beauty editor, had advised me to do once upon a time in her delightful way. But no matter what I can achieve with a blow dryer and a lipstick, I look pretty much the same.

The beautiful covering of our bodies keeps us wrapped up, contained and warm and has taken very good care of us ever since we arrived here on the Planet. We haven't always taken such good care of our skin, though. I grew up in Southern California and our after-school activity with girlfriends was to go to the beach. We didn't know the word sunblock, let alone SPF. We just went to enjoy the sun, the water, and the friendships. My mother used baby oil mixed with Iodine to get "the perfect tan." The french-fried effect.

It's quite a different thing now. We avoid the sun, as we should. But our skin is still damaged by chemicals in our water, the air we breathe, the food we ingest—and we wonder why it doesn't glow the way it used to. Once upon a time, we could use plain soap and water to achieve the youth and dewiness that we all crave. As we get older, skin care has to be an "inside job." The general approach to skincare is to put stuff on top of it. I happen to believe that we're dealing with our skin backwards.

Before you reach for that jar or sign up for that injection, I invite you to try my approach to inside-out skin care. Give it an honest week at the minimum then look in the mirror again. You may just be surprised and delighted by the woman looking back at you, smiling!

Avoid sugar, wheat, alcohol, and coffee. What!? All of those consumables are either dehydrating or are digested in such a way that the collagen in our skin becomes rigid and less bouncy.

Get out those walking shoes, put them on, and take a brisk walk. I read in the *New York Times* not too long ago about a study of exercise and middle-aged and older people led by Dr. Hiroshi Nose at the Shinshu University Graduate School of Medicine in Matsumoto, Japan. He concluded that if you walk very briskly for three minutes, then walk at a casual pace for three minutes, alternating those three minutes for a total of half an hour, it will significantly improve your aerobic fitness, leg strength, and blood pressure. I tried it and loved it. It fit into all the things that worked for me: simple clothing and walking outside. If you can't get outside or don't have the time, jump on the rebounder (the small trampoline) for lymphatic drainage for twenty minutes while you watch the news. Dry brush your skin, shower, and go!

Drink plenty of water, but not while you're eating. It dilutes your digestive enzymes.

Take your supplements and don't forget D3. When I did the play in London, I used D3 patches that I placed behind my ears. Because it was winter, there was no sun, so the patches helped tremendously.

Sleep. Oh, yes! Get it! Wallow in the time spent restoring *you*. You worked hard today. Take a shower, jump into clean sheets, and dream away. When you awake, remember to say, "Thank you!"

If surgeries and products are appealing to you, I hope you'll be careful about what you use and who does the procedures. Test any products to make sure you're not allergic. Research doctors and facilities carefully. Whatever you do, be happy about it. The cream or the procedure will not make you happy if you haven't already worked on your internal self. You don't want to come home, look in the mirror, and be scared by the woman looking back at you.

A truly happy person is not defined by her physical appearance. Of course, we all want to put our best face forward and to look in the mirror without wanting to cover it in a shroud. We all have those moments. I certainly do. I expect to see a certain reflection and have a moment of shock and panic to see something else looking back at me. But then the moment passes and I remind myself that it's just me, with the flaws and imperfections that make me unique on the planet.

An unlined forehead doesn't validate our existence as human beings. When we look at the people we cherish—children and grandchildren, friends and lovers—we don't search their faces for wrinkles and blemishes and make critical judgments. We look for clues about their health and happiness, how they feel and react to what we're saying or doing. We love their laugh lines because we helped put them there. When our loved ones look into our faces, they're not studying us for flaws, either. They see beauty far deeper than our skin.

If women can look at themselves through the eyes of the people who adore them, they can put aside their own critical eye and adore themselves. Beauty is achieved by looking at yourself with kindness, generosity, affection, and the rosy-colored lens of love . . . plus moisturizer.

SECRETS OF STAYING YOUNG—REVEALED!

Rules for looking happy and healthy at any age:

STOP COMPARING. All women are susceptible to jealousy, comparisons, and envy. Those words are detrimental to our growth and happiness. Instead of appreciating a beautiful young woman, we say, "I'm a water buffalo compared to her." Most of us will never look like a seventeen-year-old model from Slovenia, but that is the standard we are asked to achieve. Please don't compare yourself to an unobtainable ideal, your genetically gifted best friend, your daughter, or to yourself twenty years ago. Compare = despair. Despair shows on your face. Instead, embrace who you are in this moment.

BE GRATEFUL. In my travels, I've heard a lot of complaints from women about how their skin has changed, the spots and dryness. What happened to springy? Where did the dewiness go? By only seeing flaws, they forget how beautiful they are, and how beautiful it is to be alive. We're here on this planet, and not for very long. Be grateful for everything you've got, including the wrinkles.

CARE LESS. That's the real secret to great beauty, the yummiest part of life. The only person who cares if you're thin and unlined is you, and you don't have to care, either.

LATE BLOOMER

Most of my high school friends began their sexual educations at university. I was a loner for my two years at college, eating alone in my car at lunchtime, which kept me from mingling with other students or going on dates and to parties. If the right guy put the moves on me, I would have gone for it. I wasn't repressed or averse to sex for religious reasons, or any reason. It just didn't happen.

You'd think I would have been hit on by a photographer or seduced by an ad exec. But none cornered me in a fitting room. My look was Everyman's Cute Younger Sister. It must have protected me.

The first man to make an obvious pass at me was my future husband Ed. We met when I was nineteen. My agent and I were sitting in her office and she told me about a possible job at Capitol Records. She called up the art director named Ed Thrasher, and put him on speaker. "Hi, Ed," she said. "Are you still looking for a girl?"

"Yes. It's for a Billy May album. The girl is a dancer in an alley so she has to have great legs."

My agent said, "I've got someone right here. She's a brunette, tall with long legs, big brown eyes, a great smile . . ." She went on and on. I sat across the desk from her, my cheeks blazing with embarrassment.

Ed said, "If she's that great, I'll marry her."

I went over to Capitol Records. It was 5 p.m. on a Friday and the place was deserted. Not one living soul was around to point me in the right direction, so it took a while to find Ed's office. I walked in with my little portfolio. I thought, *It's dark and late. I'm alone in a huge building with a strange man.*

Ed was young—only twenty-eight—attractive, gruff. He looked through my portfolio and said, "I need to see your legs. In the flesh."

I lifted the hem of my green dress about an inch, to show my knees.

Ed said, "Higher."

"That's all you get."

He laughed and he hired me. We worked on a few album covers together and became friends. He invited me to music industry parties and I was impressed by how popular he was. Everyone wanted to be around him and his humor—witty, wry—kept people amused all night. One day, he invited me to have lunch with George Harrison and his wife at their home. At one industry house party, Bobby Darin sang "Mack the Knife" in the kitchen. Jimmy Webb performed "Up, Up and Away" at his home on a Sunday afternoon. Later on, I'd hang out with Alice Cooper and sit in the recording studio while Frank Sinatra sang "New York, New York." (Giving credit where it's due, Ed designed the cover for Frank's 1973 album and suggested the title "Ol' Blue Eyes Is Back." He ran it by Sarge, Frank's manager, who hated the title and flatly refused to discuss it with Frank. Ed persisted and eventually Sarge took the idea to the artist. The next call we got was from Sarge, saying, "I knew Frank would love it!") Later still, Ed shot the cover of Prince's *Purple Rain*.

For a girl of twenty-one who'd been pretty sheltered, hanging out with Frank Sinatra, Dean Martin, and Sammy Davis, Jr. was flat-out exciting. The artists all adored Ed because he made their albums look gorgeous. Ed charmed all of these living legends. He charmed everyone, including my parents and sister. I was receptive to his advances. We kissed a little, but didn't get far. I took it to mean he respected me. After a few months, he proposed.

My carnal knowledge thus far came from movies and what my mother told me (basically "Do what you have to do."). Sex ed? I went to a Catholic school. The only class that tangentially touched on sex was English literature and even then, we were instructed to skip over the pages of anything remotely sexual, in particular adultery, which would have made the *Scarlet Letter* read like a redacted CIA file.

So we had a lovely wedding and flew to Acapulco for our honeymoon. On the wedding night, I was twenty-one with zero experience and had no idea what to expect other than the body part mechanics. I came out of the bathroom in a pure-as-the-driven-snow ankle-length nightgown with a matching peignoir over it, and slippers with white feathery poofs on top. Ed was waiting in bed. I climbed in next to him.

Sex was a crushing disappointment. The mechanical part was what I expected, but it wasn't passionate, romantic, affectionate, or loving to say the least. The opposite.

The next morning, Ed got up before me, and said, "I'm going to go take some photos of Acapulco. See you later." He left the room and drove off in our rented Jeep. I didn't see him again until dinner.

I got out of bed and went to the mirror. I looked at my reflection, expecting to see a woman transformed. I wasn't. I stood there, wishing I felt different. I wanted to be elated, fulfilled, and joyful. Instead, I felt hollow, empty, and unloved. I had no idea what to do with myself, so I put on a bathing suit and went out to the resort's pool. I lay down on a chaise, shell-shocked, shaky, and completely alone.

As I sat there at the pool, watching the other honeymooners play and flirt, I thought, "What have I done?" I knew from night one that my marriage was not a love match. I was stuck in it, though. I'd gone from my parents' house of silent anguish into a marriage where I couldn't possibly talk about my feelings. I lacked the tools and the courage to express myself. I sensed even then that he wouldn't take me seriously, even if I could tell him how I felt. But what could I do? I was stuck. I would have to adapt and make the most of a bad situation, however I possibly could. My mother did it by drinking. I would have to find another way.

When Ed came back to the resort, we had a nice dinner and talked about nothing that really mattered. He told some funny stories about his adventure in town and we laughed together, establishing the pattern of surface interaction that would stay locked in place for decades.

I was faithful to him for all of our twenty-two years together. After the divorce, I had a lot of time to make up for. At forty-three, I started dating a musician. Sex with him was a revelation. I thought, *This is what I've been missing.* Conversation with the boyfriend wasn't as stimulating. My daughter, then fifteen, said to him, "Mom is only with you because you're great in bed." I was furious at her for saying that, but she was right (how on earth did she know?).

I proceeded to have a series of flings with creative types, musicians, writers, and artists. During the *Dallas* years, Sue Ellen and I lived parallel sex lives, both of us enjoyed the company of younger men. One of my TV boyfriends was played by Chris Atkins. I was forty-four and he was twenty-two. We filmed a scene of our characters having lunch at a coffee shop. The waitress's line was something like, "Oh, how sweet. Having a nice lunch with your son." In the scene, I was supposed to be abjectly humiliated. I remembered thinking, "Yup, this is called *acting.*" I reveled in my late-in-life sexual awakening. If you expect me to go into graphic detail, you're out of luck. My unmarried sex life has been a source of joy and pleasure for the last thirty years and I expect it to continue for the next thirty years, around which time I expect to hit my sexual peak.

We humans inhabit beautiful bodies and we should use them. The more we use them, the more beautiful we become. My sexual mantra is the classic line from *Auntie Mame:* "Life is a banquet and most poor suckers are starving to death."

Sex is sensuality, just enjoying the fact that you have a body that is wrapped, head to toe in exquisitely sensitive skin. The sensuous gift of getting older is feeling so grateful that you're not dead that you're overjoyed by every living, functioning cell and nerve ending. We only get one body. Once upon a time, I cared deeply about the clothes and jewelry I wore. Now, all I care about is my body itself—not what it looks like, but the amazing things it can do.

Our culture emphasizes only one dimension of sexuality—youth. Look at what's considered sexy in our culture. It's hard and rough. With age, those rough edges get grinded away. You become softer, and not just the hips. My whole being is gentler. I've settled softly into who I am and what turns me on. My sensuality is about making wonderful eye contact, sharing delicious conversation and luxurious silences. Younger men find women my age sexy. We are confident enough to project sensuality with our expression, our voice, our movement, and the unspoken promise of libidinous secrets to discover. We vibrate a sexual energy that they respond to.

Sophia Loren once said, "The quality of sexiness comes from within. It is something that is in you or it isn't, and it really doesn't have much to do with breasts or thighs or the pout of your lips."

When you're seventy, you're still you. Your body might look different, but you have the same need to be touched. You still care about orgasm just as much at seventy-five as you did at twenty-five. Sex can be a rich, textured, delicious natural part of your life for your whole life. If you keep healthy and avoid eating too much crap, your body will function the way it should. Your mind will send up sexy thoughts and fantasies. You'll meet a sexy man (or woman) and feel desire. He might be someone new or the same person you've been sitting across the table from for years.

BUILD A TOOL BOX

Back in 1970 if you went to a therapist, people thought you were insane. Despite the prejudice against therapy, it was the only outlet. We didn't have 800 numbers, or twenty-four-seven helplines, or the Internet, or any of the resources women can rely on today. Nowadays, people are encouraged to communicate. Instead of privately carrying an addiction, a secret, a terrible pain, now you can unburden yourself. I'm a big supporter of all the emotional tools we have today. Whatever works for you, any way you can get your stuff on the table, is better than suffering in silence as I did for way too many years.

When I first moved in with Ed, I was an eager young bride who didn't really know what I was supposed to do as a housewife. So Ed started leaving me To Do lists every day. He'd write it down on a yellow legal pad, tear off a sheet, and tape it to the fridge. Ed had beautiful handwriting, like an architect. It really was a privilege to just read the list of chores he'd assigned. At first, the lists were pretty basic. Shop for groceries. Call the plumber. Iron shirts. Polish shoes. Very simple stuff. I'd write a big check mark next to each chore after I finished it.

The list got longer and harder to tackle after we had kids and moved to the farm. Now I had chores for a whole house, family, and barn full of animals to contend with. But Ed was not deterred. He dutifully made me a list every day. While he was at the record label, I'd knock items off. When he came home at night, he walked straight to the fridge and examined my check marks.

Pointing to an unchecked item, he would ask, "You didn't do this?"

"I ran out of time," I said. "I'll do it tomorrow."

"I don't get it. What are you doing that you couldn't [take the dog to the vet, mulch the garden, etc.]?"

One day he put "paint the deck" on the list. I found the cans of paint he'd left in the garage and started the job. Our deck was pretty big and this one chore might take me all day, so I painted as fast as I could. The color was a brick red and it seemed too loud to me. But Ed was the famous art director. He was fastidious about every inch of space in the house. I got about three-quarters of the way done and really hated the color, so I stopped. I had about twenty other things to do anyway.

When Ed came home that night, he went ballistic. "What the hell is this?" he yelled at me. "This isn't the right color!"

"I used the paint you left," I said.

"Obviously there was a mistake! Why didn't you stop? How could you be so stupid?"

He complained all night that he'd have to hire someone to strip and repaint the deck because of my blunder. Ed was obviously miffed and took to writing the To Do lists in all CAPS. I responded as if I were being yelled at and scrambled to get it all done before Ed got home.

We'd been married for about ten years when, one morning, I finished my breakfast and took a look at the sheet of paper on the fridge with the list.

1. IRON MY SHIRTS.
2. WASH THE CAR.
3. FEED THE CHICKENS.

Everything else on the list became a yellow blur. I didn't want to be told what to do anymore. My resentment swelled until it was all I could think about, but instead of communicating these intense emotions, I swept them under the rug. A friend of mine knew something was wrong and insisted I go to group therapy with her.

Group therapy was a Hot! New! Trend! in 1973. It was a scene, like a singles bar, with more crying and less eye glitter. The group had about a dozen people, a good mix of ages, genders, and walks of life. I was too self-conscious to talk. In a flashback to my Dale Carnegie sessions as a teenager, the therapist asked me to hang in there and just listen. I kept going, pleased to have an excuse to get away from home one night a week.

About a month into it, I brought that day's yellow legal sheet To Do list with me to therapy and showed it to the group. They passed it around the circle. "My husband leaves this for me every day and I'm really struggling with guilt if I don't finish," I said.

An older gentleman said, "Why don't you tell him to wad up his To Do list and shove it up his ass?"

Every member of the group laid into me, asking, "Why do you put up with it?" or "What's the matter with you?" or "Can't you stand up for yourself?"

It was almost as awful as being yelled at in CAPS by Ed. But I also knew they were right and that I just needed someone to tell me that I wasn't crazy to feel such intense anger at my husband.

I started crying with relief, mainly, but I was embarrassed, too. The therapist calmed me down. As a group, we discussed the psychological, cumulative effects of spousal abuse. At first I didn't see how that applied to my situation. Ed never hit me. He'd never so much as nudged me. But the therapist explained that emotional abuse was just as destructive to self-esteem.

"Do you worry about displeasing your husband?" she asked.

"Yes."

"Do you live in fear of it?"

"Yes."

"Do you question and doubt your own judgment because you're afraid of how he'll react?"

I was textbook, before there was a textbook. Like I said, women didn't have the toolbox or readily available information at their fingertips in those days. But thanks to a concerned friend, I had group. Thank God.

"Bring him in," said the therapist. "We'll straighten him out."

"He won't come," I said.

The therapist called Ed directly. She told him I had a problem and that he needed to discuss it with the group. So he agreed to join us under the auspices that he was there to help solve my problem.

I introduced him to everyone. Instantly, the men turned on him. The little old man said, "How dare you treat her like that?"

They went 'round the circle, lambasting Ed. I was shaking the whole time and he was visibly vibrating with insult and fury. The drive home was not pretty.

"You sandbagged me!" he rightly accused.

I said, "I didn't know they'd do that," although I knew perfectly well and had been fantasizing about how it'd go down for days. The group did my dirty work and Ed was humiliated. I finally had some rudimentary tools in my box. I used group like a hammer.

Despite Ed's dismissal of his one and only therapy session, he got the message. The daily To Do list disappeared. But the subtle cruelty continued. As was his style, he made a joke of it and started leaving blank yellow legal pads around the house, on my pillow, in the bathroom. They were little reminders, or warnings, that the pads still lurked. At any time, he could write on one, tear off a sheet, and tape it to the fridge.

During my consciousness-raising, I read *The Yellow Wallpaper*, by Charlotte Perkins Gilman, about an emotionally abused woman with a controlling husband who believed the yellow wallpaper in her room was coming to life and attacking her. The character didn't get out with her mind intact. If I hadn't pushed the issue at group, I might've lost my own mind over The Yellow Legal Pad Paper. Now I look back and laugh at how afraid I was of spotting those yellow rectangles around the house.

With all that practice, I became a fastidious To Do list maker in my own right, almost picking up the habit for myself after Ed dropped it. I even use the same pads he once did. If he were alive, Ed might be amused that I'm writing this book, these very words, on a sheet of yellow legal paper. I find it pretty hilarious.

EXPLORE UNDISCOVERED ROADS

Right after we got back from our honeymoon, I couldn't help noticing that Ed kept popping Mylanta pills into his mouth. I had no idea just how bad his acid reflux was—or "nervous stomach" as he called it. Ed couldn't go an hour without a Mylanta. I'd find empty blister packs all over the house. I insisted he go to a doctor, who told him to keep doing what he was doing.

"For how long?" I asked.

"The rest of my life," he said.

He was only twenty-eight. It was inconceivable that he'd pop those pills all day long for the next fifty years. He was oddly accepting of the doctor's prognosis. But I wasn't. I thought, *I'll find a cure!* Ed grew up eating heavy stuff, gravy and steaks. I grew up eating light, picking fresh fruit off the backyard tree (often because that was the only snack option available). I was sure Ed's diet of grease and starch was to blame for his problems.

"We're going to change your eating habits and see what happens," I announced.

At the time, we were living in a little guest house in Studio City, a suburb of Los Angeles. The efficiency kitchen was going to be my laboratory. First I went to the library and read up on the subject, devouring books by Paavo Airola, the 1960s version of Mehmet Oz, and Adelle Davis, the first lady of nutrition and inventor of granola. Both of these doctors swore by the power of food as medicine. With dreams of being the best wife I could be, I made some strict changes.

Out: white bread, gravy, grease, red meat.

In: fresh fruit and vegetables, fish, chicken. Pretty much the same way I ate before I got married and still eat now.

After a few days, Ed said, "I feel better."

In fact, when he went back in for a checkup a month later, his symptoms were nearly gone. The doctor asked, "What did you do?"

Ed said, "My wife is making me eat vegetables."

"Well, keep it up. You don't have to take those pills anymore."

It was the validation equivalent of a medical school diploma. I was high-fiving myself before high-fives existed. Cooking became an obsession. Whenever I wasn't working, I was studying about the power of food. Reading dense texts about nutrition required more brainpower than shampooing my hair on camera at work or changing diapers at home. I loved my kids, but I was craving something more. I needed mental stimulation and found it by becoming an expert on this subject, one that deeply impacted my own family.

We were living in Encino and I would take the kids in their stroller to the local health food store. The kids drank fresh carrot juice while I shopped for my organic ingredients. I always chatted a bit with the store owner, a tiny woman from Tennessee named Gerry. California was the epicenter of the burgeoning organic food craze, but Gerry was no hippie. She was just a sweet Southern lady who really, really cared about hummus.

"Hi, Linda!" she'd say. "We have fresh tofu today!"

"Fresh tofu? Wherever did you get it?"

Back then bricks of tofu were as precious at bars of gold. It was a rare luxury and not a food staple found at nearly every highway gas station Qwik-Mart like it is today (at least in California). Gerry and I shot the breeze a few times a week for years, conversations that started like this: "Don't you just love tabouleh?" and "I don't know what my life would be like without carob."

A QUICK WORD FROM THE NUTRITION NUT

The subject of weight and food comes up whenever I speak to women about their lives. Regarding what I eat, I always mention my favorite quote from author Michael Pollan: "Eat food. Not too much. Mostly plants." My rules are to keep it clean, simple, and true. If you're over-weight, eat less. If you're too thin, eat more. Be sure to eat the best quality that you can afford, hopefully organic. No more excuses. Stop the constant dialogue of blaming someone, a circumstance, or your genes. You know exactly what you're choosing to put in your mouth. Choose wisely.

Since the number one question I've been asked by reporters over the years is, "What do you eat for breakfast?" I thought I'd finally give a decent answer. Here is the healthy, organic way I start each day: I begin by drinking a cleansing cup of warm lemon water as I prepare my breakfast smoothie and cook up an egg and vegetable dish.

Lemon Water

Ingredients
juice of 1/2 a lemon
1 cup of hot water

Instructions: Squeeze the lemon juice into the hot water. Enjoy.

Breakfast Smoothie

Ingredients

2 handfuls of spinach, chard, or another green

1 tablespoon chia seeds

1 tablespoon flaxseeds (They must be freshly ground because they
turn rancid very fast.)

1 tablespoon maca or cacao

1 stalk celery

1 cucumber

juice of $1/2$ a lemon

1 square inch ginger

a sprig of fresh parsley

a sprig of fresh cilantro

1 piece of fruit of your choice (I use $1/2$ a frozen banana; or berries or
a green apple are all the sweet you need in a veggie smoothie)

1 cup almond milk (see recipe for homemade below)

1 serving hemp protein powder

Instructions: Put all the ingredients in a Vitamix or a NutriBullet
(which I prefer to a juicer because they retain the fiber). Blend. Enjoy.

Almond Milk

Ingredients

2 cups raw almonds

5 cups filtered water

1 seed bag (purchase at health food store or Amazon)

Instructions: Cover almonds with water and soak overnight. In the
morning, pour off the water, rinse, and put in blender or Vitamix. Add
about three cups of fresh water and blend until smooth. Place a seed
bag in a bowl, dump the almond water mixture into the seed bag,
and start squeezing. It's sort of like milking a cow! Keep squeezing to
get all the liquid out of the bag. If you like, add a few drops of Stevia
English Toffee.

Eggs and Spinach

Ingredients

$^1/_2$ pound of triple-rinsed organic spinach (try to buy organic, especially veggies; nothing tastes quite like them)

2 eggs

1 tablespoon coconut oil or grass-fed butter (unsalted)

1 ounce feta cheese

salt and pepper to taste

Instructions: In a large pan, sauté the spinach in coconut oil or butter. In another pan, either poach (use a tablespoon of vinegar in the water so the egg holds its shape) or scramble eggs in coconut oil or butter. Lay the eggs on top of sautéed spinach and crumble cheese on top. Add salt and pepper to taste.

Goji Berries and Pumpkin Seeds

My version of trail mix. I always have a baggie of it in my purse for energy. You can buy goji berries and organic pumpkin seeds at any health food store. Or go to dragonherbs.com to buy my favorite brand.

NOW, BACK TO THE SEVENTIES...

. . . when everyone was high on pot, except me. I had babies to care for. I loved the fashion, though, the long, flowing skirts and hair. I dressed like a flower child, with actual flowers in my hair. It was a great time to be alive in California. Everyone seemed to be searching for answers. Many of my friends were going to ashrams and seeking out gurus to help them along their spiritual path. Me? I was too busy to go to an ashram, but I was inspired by the times. It started with organic foodstuffs, and reading about nutrition. That led to more research and more mental exploration. If I'd stayed in college, I might've learned about philosophy and religions there. But I dropped out. I had to teach it all to myself.

Mark Twain once said, "The two most important days of your life are the day you were born and the day you find out why." During the early years of my marriage and motherhood, I felt a hole open up inside. I had a sense that if I didn't fill that hole, I'd soon become the kind of woman who wore gold necklaces, started drinking at breakfast, and watched her life go by in a lonely, miserable blur.

I was connecting to my childhood and my young adulthood through my mother. I'd seen what an unfulfilled life looked like and I knew that growing up that way had affected me deeply. I wanted to be a wonderful mother, but I didn't have a role model. I wanted to be a better person and therefore a better mother. I had the presence of mind to see that somehow, I'd set up my own life to be frighteningly similar to my mother's and feared becoming like her. This was the hole I'd dug for myself.

How to get out of it? I started searching for answers, just like my guru and ashram-going friends. I went from walking the aisle at Gerry's and searching in the library to browsing in esoteric bookstores. Books became my solace. I was eager to find out who I was in the grand scheme of things. One book led to another. They inflamed my thirst for knowledge and inner knowing. I was reading all the time and questioning, thirsting for expansion. These mental explorations were the beginning steps of figuring out who I was, what I wanted, how I could be of value, and how to serve, apart from my family.

The hole inside me went from being the problem to being the solution. I came to call it the Rabbit Hole. I fell into it. My curiosity propelled me forward. Each book took me deeper into it and opened new avenues to explore. Some of the titles I devoured in the '70s and still reread today that expanded and enhanced my thinking and life are *Autobiography of a Yogi* by Paramhansa Yogananda and *Zen Mind, Beginner's Mind* by Shunryu Suzuki.

Books were an escape from my wife/mother routine and they were my passion. I read and learned new ideas and practices, including meditation and prayer. Being silent and asking for peace and help took me places and opened my intuition and heart.

As my heart opened up, things started flying open and deepening at the same time. People came into my life who were absolutely perfect for where I was at a particular time and place in my development. Gerry, the friendly organic grocer, would play an important part in my life, as you'll soon read.

If I hadn't spent five years reading books that urged me to seek my own path, to look inward for personal satisfaction, to know the power of patience as well as the power of inspiration, I might have sunk into my life as it was, my mom's life, and never believed that I could aspire to more. It was a transformative lesson—just realizing I had a right, an obligation to pursue a creative path—was the first step on it.

Most women collect shoes. I collect books! Each of these books came into life with absolute perfect timing when I needed the message it offered the most. If any of these titles jumps out at you, you might need to read it for where you are in your life. I recommend all of them for your metaphysical book clubs.

Meditations for Women Who Do Too Much by Anne Wilson Schaef
Search Inside Yourself by Chado-Meng Tan
My Inventions by Nikola Tesla
Quantum Healing by Deepak Chopra
You Can Heal Your Life by Louise Hay
Second Sight by Judith Orloff
A Woman's Worth by Marianne Williamson
Sanctuary by Stephen Lewis and Evan Slawson
The Beauty Myth by Naomi Wolf
Daring Greatly by Brene Brown
Power vs. Force by David Hawkin
The Four Agreements by Don Miguel Ruiz and Janet Mills
The Seat of the Soul by Gary Zukov
A New Earth by Eckart Tolle

CAT HEAVEN

Twenty years ago, the best friend I ever had walked into my life and never left.

He appeared in the yard, a kitten, only a couple of months old. I scooped him up and took him to the vet to check him out and ask if anyone had reported a missing cat. The vet said, "I haven't heard anything. But I will tell you one thing, Linda. This little guy loves you."

The tuxedo kitten with four white paws had buried his head in the crook of my elbow. I looked at him and said, "So it's like that, is it?"

I named him Dugu and called him Dugie. I spoiled him rotten, cooking chicken breast for him or buying bison to feed him raw. He expected his breakfast at 6 a.m. and I, his humble servant, arrived to do his bidding.

He was elegant, always dressed in a tux. And he knew to stand up when a lady entered the room. We traveled well together. In our Dallas condo, he loved to look out the window, twenty-two stories high. We'd gone from a sprawling country house with ready access to the outdoors, to living in a two-bedroom condo high-rise. We both appreciated the change in scenery. At night, we'd go out on the terrace together and look at the lights of the skyline. It was so different from the canyon house in Los Angeles. We'd nod at each other and agree. Change is good.

A lover of simple things, Dugie was well groomed. His tux and shoes were always immaculate. Independent like me, he preferred his own company to anyone else's, except mine. We would do our morning walk around the pool and garden together. At the ranch, when I sat outside on a chaise, he'd sun with me and jump down to drink water out of the pool. I'd find him staring into my koi pond, drinking the water, but he never laid a paw on the fish. Not once. He loved to watch them, just like I did.

We slept together for twenty years. I would say, "Snoozies!" and he'd charge down the hallway and make a flying leap on the bed. We watched TV, cuddling. We held hands, his paw in mine, as he slept. I was the big spoon.

A wise kitty, he would look at my shoes to know what I had planned that day. If I wore my running shoes, he'd wait by the door for me. If I wore slippers, he'd jump into bed. If I had on high heels, he'd curl up on the couch until I got home. If I wore flats and had luggage, he'd turn his back on me, sad and angry. I would always tell him that I'd be coming home soon.

Then it was his turn to leave and I knew he wasn't coming back.

Ideally, you make your final exit in peace and love.

The day before, I knew something was wrong. Dugie looked at me like he wanted something, but he wouldn't eat his bison or anchovies. In bed that night, we spooned, but before I woke up, he'd gone to his hiding place behind the big chair in the bedroom. I found him at dawn and lay on the sheepskin next to him. We talked about all of our adventures and how much fun we'd had together. Then I took him out to the grass under the oak tree, the same place I had found him twenty years ago, and we said good-bye. I didn't cry until he was gone, and didn't stop for a long, long time after. I am crying right now, writing these words, thinking about his little face.

Eckhart Tolle once said, "I have lived with many Zen masters, all of them cats." I'm with you, Eckhart! There is no such thing as a "crazy cat lady." Loving and sharing your life with a cat is the sanest thing a human being can do.

I still wait to let Dugie in at night. I still look for him lounging by the pool with his elegant, sophisticated ennui. And I still see his little body by the oak tree where he chose me, where my soul chose him, and where he took his last breath. He was my therapist, my love, my Zen master, and my dearest friend. He is so dearly missed.

LEARN TO NAVIGATE
FOR YOURSELF

Ed's dream was to be a cowboy. He fantasized about family life on the frontier circa 1888, living off the fat of the land. He art directed his vision every year for our family photo Christmas card. He picked our *Little House on the Prairie* wardrobes, styled our hair and makeup, and designed the set. We posed around the wagon wheel.

When he pushed to move from suburban Encino to a plot of dirt in Canyon Country, I balked. It was pretty far out there, forty-five minutes from downtown L.A., a patch of nothing miles from the nearest store, restaurant, or paved road. He convinced me to give it a try. We sampled country life camping in my father's Airstream trailer on the weekends. The trailer had been our summer vacation home when I was growing up. We'd drive to the beach or the mountains and spend weekends in it. Those were happy memories from childhood and it was nice to revisit them with my own family. The trailer had a table that folded down from the wall. I could open the oven and put food on the table without getting up from the seat. I felt very proud of myself for making recipes from *Sunset* magazine in that teeny, tiny kitchen. The kids loved it. Ed was beside himself. He argued that all that weekend camping fun could be ours every day of the week. I was wary. Moving would take me so far away from Betty and my parents and all my friends. But as an accommodating wife, I reluctantly agreed.

The plan was to build a dream house from scratch. Ed gave me free reign and I took it. I wasn't happy about moving so far from my family, but if it were going to happen, I'd turn it into an educational project. I went into full-force research mode. I headed for the library and found information about a wealthy woman who'd designed her own country house. One of the details she invented was to have all the house light controls wired into her panel in her bedroom, so she could turn on and off every light in the house from her bed. I loved that idea. When Ed traveled, I'd be alone with two kids in the country. If I woke up one night and heard lions, tigers, and elephants rampaging outside, I could flip on the security lights in a flash. My research for the building plans focused my thoughts and mental energy. If I hadn't been so busy dealing with architects and contractors, I would have fallen into a depression about having to live way out there. The building research—like my nutrition research and campaign to break into talkie commercials—consumed my mind, satisfied my creativity, and helped me deal.

Our house rose from the dirt like a desert flower. The picture wasn't complete without a barn, which we built, and filled with animals. I bought Ed a horse for his birthday. He was ecstatic with his gift. Wearing a cowboy hat and boots, Ed would take Dusty on long rides in the canyon on weekends. I didn't mind. It was like being a golf widow.

Next we bought Granger, my horse. He took verbal instructions like a teen model. I could say, "Walk!" or "Canter!" and he'd do it. Granger and I had a special love. I'd ride him into the hills and tell him my problems. His ears would twitch, waiting for a command word he understood, and then he'd comply. It was sweet how much he wanted to make me happy.

The barn was alive with dogs, cats, a pig named Bacon, and a dozen chickens. I gave them hennish names like Lillian, Helen, and Beatrice, but I had to stop. The first lesson of farm life: Do not name the chickens. You'll get too attached. Coyotes would snatch them out of the coop at night. In the morning, we'd find scattered feathers. Every time we lost one, it broke my heart.

Ed's dream house continued to evolve. He'd say, "We need a pool" or "We need a tennis court." So I'd go out and get a TV commercial to pay for it. Noxzema built our pool. VO5 upgraded our stables. Hanes paid for the tennis court. One national TV ad could bring in $30,000 a year in residuals, which was a lot of money back in the '70s. With the kids, house, and animals, Ed didn't think it was a good idea for me to work full-time. He never said, "You may not work." But the implication was clear. I designed the house; Ed designed our life.

My years as a homestead housewife were busy and full. We did everything as a family. After we put in the pool, it was the hub of summer activity. Friends and neighbors came over and the summers were always filled with parties and barbecues. The pool made us very popular in the neighborhood. We shared everything with our new friends and I started to feel like the move wasn't a bad idea.

The tennis court gave us another opportunity to do things as a family. We played crazy family foursomes and got pretty good actually. We had tournaments with trophies and played in teams, always mixing it up. The kids got so good on the court that we sent them to tennis camp in Big Bear, where Ed had spent time as a kid. When they came back, they were far too good. Ed and I didn't stand a chance against them. They loved to beat the crap out of us, and we were proud of how talented they were.

Jeff loved to be on his bike in the hills out back and took over a huge part of the backyard to build the ultimate bike course. He used

the tractor to dig holes for ponds and his jumps. It was a BMX ex-
travaganza, which brought all the neighborhood boys to our place for
most weekends and after-school fun. He is now an accomplished cy-
clist (those guys who wear spandex) and that is his love.

By 1976 when I was thirty-six, I'd been entertaining the neighborhood, raising the kids, feeding the chickens, and slopping the pig for
ten years. The charms of country life were wearing thin. Yes, I loved
the pool and the tennis court. I adored my horse. But all that came
with it—mucking horseshit at 6 a.m., the cooking and cleaning, caring for a dozen creatures—wasn't personally fulfilling. I was exhausted
and had no time or energy for myself.

The concept of "Me Time" hadn't been invented yet. I lacked the
verbal skills to explain how trapped I felt in a life of chores. Ed had a
limited tolerance for discussing my feelings. I was supposed to be the
tough as nails pioneer wife who could kill a varmint, birth a baby, and
churn a pound of butter before dawn. It was the only version of me he
cared to see. When I pushed back, Ed would mock my complaints. He
had a sharp wit. Very sharp. I was cowed by it. But it didn't stop me.

I went to the library and researched acting classes in L.A. One
night after the kids had gone to bed, Ed and I were sitting at the dining
room table. I said, "I want to enroll in an acting workshop."

"No. The kids need you at home. Wait until they're in college to
take a class."

Thud. His words landed on the table like a rock. I wasn't even
angry. I was stunned. He felt entitled to forbid me from taking a class?
It made me feel less than human, like Ed's appendage. For ten years
my life had been about fulfilling his dreams and now he was telling me
he wanted ten more. Wait until the kids were in college to start acting? I'd be in my mid-forties by then, when most women's Hollywood
careers ended.

I got up from the table without saying a word and left the room. I
didn't know what else to do. Ed went back to his coffee. The subject

had been raised, swatted down, and that was that as far as he was concerned.

I walked outside, struggling for air. A band tightened around my chest. I thought, *I'm never getting out of here.* Like my precious chickens, I was trapped in a cage. Like my beloved horse, I was trained to obey simple commands. Cook. Clean. Repeat. Ed and I didn't argue or fight. We never talked about money, sex, or parenting. We just did what he wanted, no further discussion. I was as voiceless as the animals I cared for.

A few years earlier, psychotherapist Arthur Janov's landmark book *Primal Scream* came out and gained a wide following in Southern California. The practice was to relive and release deep childhood trauma vocally, by emitting a cry of anguish. Some of my friends were doing it and gave the therapy rave reviews. I didn't get how screaming was healing. Where did the scream come from? How could you tap into it?

That night, a sound grew in my head, a siren cry, that got louder and louder, like an approaching ambulance. It wasn't something I could vocalize like a primal scream. It was a private scream that blared a dire warning in my skull. Unless I responded to the emergency, I would disappear and there'd be nothing left of me but a few feathers.

The very next day, I enrolled in acting lessons at the famous CEC Studio in Burbank. I didn't make a big deal of it at home. I used our marital code of silence to my advantage and sprung the news on Ed. On the way out the door to my first class, I said, "I'm going to Burbank now for my acting workshop. I'll be home in a few hours." And then I just left. Ed would have had to physically restrain me in front of the kids to keep me at home and that was not his style.

Just like the Dale Carnegie course, our workshop began by going around the room and introducing ourselves to each other.

"Hi, I'm Dee Wallace," said a pixieish blonde who would one day play Elliot's mother in *E.T.: The Extra-Terrestrial.*

"I'm Carl Weathers," said the future Apollo Creed.

"I'm Susan Blakely," said the adorable girl next door, soon to be the sensation of the TV miniseries *Rich Man, Poor Man*.

"I'm Veronica Hamel," said the stunning blue-eyed brunette, the future star of *Hill Street Blues*. In a few years, the two of us would be up against each other for an Emmy, and lose to Veronica's cast mate Barbara Babcock.

Our workshop was like *Battle of the Network Stars: Before They Were Stars: Bicentennial Edition*. I was the oldest one there by at least ten years. Most of the students were in their early twenties or late teens, just arrived in Los Angeles. After class they'd go out for coffee or they went to work. I'd go home and relieve the babysitter.

Our coach was Charles E. Conrad, a legend. He taught us the eponymous Conrad Method of memorizing scripts by repeating the lines really fast over and over again to desensitize yourself to them. Then, when we got to doing a scene with other actors, we wouldn't have preconceptions about how to play it. The objective was to react to the words like we'd never heard them before, feeling the emotion beneath them and reacting spontaneously to your scene partner. You know the cliché, "Acting is reacting!" Charles Conrad said it first.

One day I was doing a scene with another student. Charles pulled me to the side and said, "Take the glass of water on the table and throw it in his face." I did it. The entire class gasped. The purpose was to get a reaction. It worked. (In good time, I'd become an expert at throwing water in someone's face. It was Sue Ellen's signature move.) We got close in that room, and were always encouraging and supportive.

Meanwhile, back at the ranch . . .

Ed grimly accepted my taking the class. I'd have a ball there, improvising a volcanic marital spat with Carl Weathers, and then come home to Ed's disapproving silence. How could two people live together, isolated in the country, sleep in the same bed, eat at the same table, without speaking of anything that really mattered? My parents were the same way. In the twenty-one years I lived in their house, I never once witnessed my parents talk about anything important, like money, or marriage, or Mom's alcoholism, or happiness. They had their roles, their scripts, their marks, and they hit them over and over, every day. If Dad had a problem with Mom, he didn't say a word about it. He accepted his evening cocktail. He ate the food I cooked, listened to his Ella Fitzgerald records, went to bed, and started all over again. Mom's life seemed to pass in a blur.

Divorce was not a viable option for me. Good Catholic girls did not leave their husbands. I just turned my attention away from my husband, toward my children and the class. I went through the motions at home and purged years of suppressed emotions in class.

Interestingly, by attending acting workshop, I became an equal part in it. The kids would come home, bubbling about something that happened at school. Ed would have a story to tell about his day. And then, it'd be my turn to tell a story about a funny moment in class. I realized that unless you have something of value to share from outside the relationship, you can't be an equal partner inside it. This simple truth was revelatory. It made me feel warmly toward Ed, just for listening.

After a few glasses of wine one night, he said, "I hate this. If you care at all about our marriage, you'll stop."

I said, "What do you think is going to happen? That I'll run off with Marcello Mastroianni?" I happened to have a huge crush on the Italian actor.

"Of course not!" he said. But maybe he was a little afraid.

"I love the class. I'm not quitting," I said.

He scowled at me and said, "I hope nothing ever comes of it."

At least he was honest.

Another year went by and I landed a couple of tiny parts, including the nurse on *Marcus Welby, M.D.* I was so terrified the night before, I grinded my teeth into an abscess. Half of my face ballooned up. The makeup artist arranged my hair to cover my swollen cheek and masterfully shaded my chin to give it definition. Ed sent a bedpan full of flowers to the set, which the other "nurses" thought was so clever and sweet. I was thrown for a loop. It was an about-face for him. I hoped that it meant he was inclining toward supporting me and my work. My heart expanded. Instead of talking, which he didn't know how to do, he sent a thoughtful, funny gift.

My next job came about in a surprising way. Remember Gerry? The organic food lady? One day in 1977, Gerry and I were chatting about the produce and she asked casually, "So, Linda, what do you do?"

We usually didn't talk about our personal lives. I said, "I'm a mom and model, and I'm taking acting classes. I'm trying to get work, but it's not easy."

"Oh! You should call my husband!"

I thought, *Right.* Everyone in Los Angeles has some tangential connection to the entertainment biz. Her husband was probably the second unit director for some small production company.

To be polite, I asked, "Who's your husband?"

She said, "Dennis Weaver!"

"*McCloud* Dennis Weaver?" For those of you who don't remember or weren't yet born, *McCloud* was a detective drama about a cowboy transplanted in the mean streets of Manhattan, and a smash hit. Dennis Weaver in his cowboy hat, sheep fleece coat, and slow southern drawl was a thinking woman's sex symbol. I was shocked that tiny, sweet Gerry was the wife of six-foot-tall tough guy Dennis Weaver.

"I'm writing down his secretary's number. When you call her, tell her I sent you."

I could hear that conversation now. "Um, hello, my name is Linda. I know Dennis's wife from the health food store. I mentioned that I love acting, so she told me to give him a . . ." *Click.*

I fully expected to get hung up on. But I called anyway. Sure enough, the secretary/gatekeeper said, "Mr. Weaver is *very* busy. He can give you five minutes three weeks from Thursday."

I said, "Great! See you then!" In the meantime, I sent over my headshots and my résumé, just so the secretary knew I was verging on legit.

I went to Universal Studios for the appointment, right on time. The secretary said, "He has ten minutes and then you have to leave." I walked in for my one-on-one meeting with TV's biggest star.

He was taller and even more handsome than I expected. "So you know my wife from the store," he said. So charming! He was exactly as he seemed on the show. Genuine, confident, and adorable.

"Yes," I said. "Best granola clusters in California."

So we started talking and I ended up staying for two hours. He took out the guitar and sang a song his son had written. The whole time, I kept waiting for the ejector button.

Eventually he did have to throw me out, but he was gentle. I thanked him for seeing me and left. If nothing more, I had a great story to tell my friends.

Two weeks later, I went on an audition. I read a one-sided phone call ("Hello? Yes? What's that? An accident? Oh my God! Was anyone hurt! No! No! Not little Billy!" or something like that) and was hired on the spot. Dennis liked how I did on that one scene and hired me later to guest-star in a two-hour Christmas special that Dennis himself was directing. When I gushed my appreciation to him later, he said, "I saw something in you." What he saw in me were fifteen years' worth of his wife's food.

My next big job was on Norman Lear's *All That Glitters* playing Linda Murkland, a male-to-female transsexual. Norman said, "You're perfect for the part." I didn't know how to take it. The concept of the show was to turn gender roles upside down. Women were in power. The men—including *WKRP in Cincinnati*'s Gary Sandy—were hapless flunkies. The cast included David Dukes, Barbara Baxley, and Jessica Walter, all fabulous people. It was a real incubator. My character was kidnapped by farmers who locked her in the chicken coop, an all-too-familiar metaphor for me. In one scene, a chicken sat on my lap and laid an egg, an unfortunate harbinger for the show. It aired for thirteen weeks and was cancelled.

Ed was thrilled. He said, "Well, you tried. Now you can be at home full-time again."

The scream flared up. I reacted to it by taking more classes and staying in touch with industry people, including a makeup artist from *All That Glitters*. He also worked at *The Man From Atlantis*, starring heartthrob Patrick Duffy. I was dying to meet him.

One day, the makeup artist and I were going to lunch and he told me he had to drop something off on the way. We pulled up to a lovely house in Hollywood, knocked on the door, and there was the Webbed Wonder himself with his wife and two boys. I was completely star-struck. (It always irked Larry Hagman that Patrick and I met each other first.)

I heard through the grapevine that casting agent Ruth Conforte was working on a show called *Dallas*. Brunette Victoria Principal was already in as Pam Ewing, and they wanted a blonde to play her sister-in-law, Sue Ellen. The first choice was Mary Frann, a dear friend, who later was the wife on *Newhart*.

Ruth knew me from *All That Glitters* and convinced the show creator, David Jacobs, and producer Philip Capice to see me, despite my being a brunette. The audition was another one-sided phone call. David had written the audition scene. We'd done a lot of them at CEB Studio. It was right in my wheelhouse.

David said, "Your husband is calling to tell you he won't be home for your son's birthday because he has business." Oh, yeah, that old excuse.

I reacted to David reading J.R.'s end of the conversation. I thanked them and left. Start to finish, the audition took five minutes. When I got in my car, I turned on the ignition, and I just knew. My women's intuition was on fire. My life was about to change.

The night of the scream, I learned two crucial life skills: (1) always listen to my subconscious when it yells at me, and (2) acting and reacting aren't craft, they're survival. Acting means doing what it takes to protect yourself. Reacting keeps you alive in a threatening situation. If I hadn't heeded the warning and openly rebelled against my husband, I would have lost the will to go on. I did what I had to do to survive. I know that sounds dramatic, but I felt like I was fighting for my life.

We all shake our heads when people are told to evacuate but choose to ride out the storm to their peril. But many of us ride out storms to our peril in our own lives, be they abusive partners, addictions, a job that makes us miserable, preventable health conditions. It can seem easier to ignore the warnings than take action. I've known plenty of women who despised their husbands, but refused to leave. Some women have told me over the years that Sue Ellen inspired them to ditch the J.R.s in their lives. One told me, "Instead of praying for him to die, I saved myself." I'm proud of her and of whatever I might have done as an actor to inspire her.

Philosopher Friedrich Nietzsche said, "Enjoy life. This is not a dress rehearsal." On the road to happiness, one must be aware that we are living our one and only life each and every second. If this really were your last day, you'd want to spend it with someone, or doing something, you love. Don't ask permission. Don't wait until next week. Just go out there and get it.

TOUGH LOVE

Sue Ellen Ewing was a mogul's wife with the shiny outside and a pickled liver. My main acting challenge would be to hover in the background and get quietly sloshed while Patrick Duffy and Victoria Principal emoted all over each other. If I moved to the foreground of the scene, it'd be to refresh my fake drink. On the plus side, I would stay well hydrated on set.

One of my pet peeves about actors playing drunk was going over the top, stumbling around, knocking things off the furniture, slurring their words, and rolling their eyes. Sue Ellen was a millionaire's wife and former beauty queen and would rather die than look sloppy. Her number one job was to present a shellacked, classy image to the world while struggling to hold onto her last shreds of dignity. She might look the part, but she was always one sip away from mayhem.

Ever the list maker and homework doer, I started researching how to play a sneaky drunk. I asked friends and my former coach, Charles Conrad, for tips. I read up on the subject and screened some movies for inspiration. The 1966 film version of Edward Albee's *Who's Afraid of Virginia Woolf?* is a master class on how to act progressively wasted and I marveled at the skill and control of Elizabeth Taylor and Sandy Dennis. The best tip I found was from a book by Uta Hagen. Her trick was to cross your eyes ever so slightly, not so anyone would notice, but enough to blur your focus slightly. It worked brilliantly. When I reached for something, it wasn't quite where it was supposed to be. It forced me to slow down and make my movements deliberate. Drunks craved the effects of alcohol while constantly fighting to hide them. Every drink contained an internal battle with shame as a garnish.

April 1, 1978: The Gerald Ford family staged an intervention for Betty Ford, former First Lady, at their home in Rancho Mirage, California, to convince her to submit to a week of alcohol and drug detox under the supervision of doctors.

April 2, 1978: *Dallas* premiered, including a scene of Sue Ellen chugging a glass of vodka during the family's regular cocktail hour.

April 12, 1978: *The New York Times* reported that Betty Ford had checked into the Navy hospital in Long Beach for "overmedication."

April 29, 1978: The *Times* quoted Mrs. Ford saying, "I'm addicted to alcohol." She would stay in the Navy hospital to rehab and learn the 12 Steps of Alcoholics Anonymous for another month.

March 23, 1979: J.R. committed pregnant Sue Ellen to a sanitarium against her will to force her to dry out.

October 4, 1982: The Betty Ford Center opened in Rancho Mirage.

Dallas and Betty Ford's admission and recovery from alcoholism overlapped in real time. She put it all out there like no first lady had done before. Her breast cancer announcement alone broke ground. In the '70s people still whispered "the C word," and no one would dare say "breast" in public. Betty Ford followed up a year later, by telling the world that while living in the White House and sleeping next to the leader of the free world, she was taking painkillers with alcohol. She had no idea she had a problem. As Ford said later in life, "My makeup wasn't smeared, I wasn't disheveled, I behaved politely, and I never finished off a bottle, so how could I be an alcoholic?"

Incredibly, the *Times* buried the "overmedication" story on page eight. Her declaration that she was an addict appeared on page fourteen. How would the news break today, if, say, Laura Bush had announced that while her husband was invading Iraq, she was plowing through the White House wine cellar? It'd be front-page news around the globe! Barbara Walters interviewed an inebriated Betty Ford in the White House in 1976 and cut the footage to protect the First Lady. In those days, even journalists swept addiction under the rug.

Betty Ford's name is now synonymous with recovery. Her legacy is having the courage to take her addiction out of the closet. God bless her for opening the clinic that saved so many lives. As impressive as her bravery was, I applaud her children and husband for staging the intervention, not a common practice at the time. Families were far more likely to ignore a problem rather than confront it and deal with it.

Sue Ellen's drinking wasn't a major plotline on *Dallas* at first. But when the Mrs. Ford story unfolded, Sue Ellen's struggle was suddenly culturally relevant. It also resonated with viewers on a personal level. During the Cold War era, social drinking was acceptable behavior, especially among housewives. They'd have wine with lunch or cocktails after shopping, a drink when their husband came home, and another two or three during dinner. Sue Ellen drank to break the tedium of her sheltered life. She anesthetized herself to dull the pain of unrealized dreams and a loveless marriage. She felt trapped in her life and vodka gave her a temporary escape. Not many viewers shared Sue Ellen's pampered lifestyle. But they related to pouring a shot of vodka into their OJ at breakfast and mixing a cocktail before the kid got home from school.

So many people have told me over the years that they found the courage to admit they had a problem thanks to Sue Ellen. During the run of the show, many friends asked me confidentially, "Is it normal to have a bottle of wine every night at dinner?" The show was over the top, of course. We weren't going for reality. Somewhere at the center of all those soap opera bubbles was a kernel of truth. People recognized Sue Ellen's drinking in themselves and in members of their families.

I personally know many people who went to AA because of *Dallas*. Even colleagues, people who shouldn't have confided their private habits to me, felt emboldened to confess. "I see you on the show and you're doing exactly what I did for decades," said one friend, a man in a very powerful position, a decision maker who appeared, to all the world, in complete control. He went to AA and changed his life. Who knows what might've happened to him if he hadn't gotten help? Or to the First Lady? Or to my mother?

Marge, my mother, was born in 1918, the same year as Betty Ford, a member of the Greatest Generation. It was an era of duty and toughness, when personal problems were best kept to oneself. In her teens, Marge was a ballerina, and then in her twenties she became a fashion illustrator and designer. I failed to appreciate her talent growing up. While cleaning out her house after she died, I found a book of her illustrations. Her aesthetic was very Andrews Sisters: big rows of buttons, sleek dresses, and high-waisted tap pants. Paging through the book, I felt proud of her talent. Sewing pinafores and decorating the window display in Dad's jewelry store couldn't have come close to satisfying her creative needs. If she'd been born in 1958 instead of 1918, Marge might've become Donna Karan. But as a woman of her time, Marge was expected to be a homemaker. Frustration, boredom, and squashed dreams fueled her heavy drinking.

The Betty Fords and Betty Drapers of the '50s and '60s could help themselves to a glass of gin as the mood struck and no one would have raised an eyebrow. Cocktail hour was a flexible term. A classic ad at the time was of a wife handing her husband a cocktail as soon as he walked through the front door. My parents liked gimlets, vodka and lime juice in a pretty glass. Dad would stop after one or two. But each night, Mom wore down the carpet between the couch and the wet bar. She was probably going there during the day, too, when we were at school. Mom's personality changed as the evening wore on. She'd blur around the edges, until she'd look at us like we weren't there. As a kid, it was terrifying to watch. But we never, ever talked about it. As I grew up, I reacted like a lot of children of alcoholics and became a good girl. I wouldn't touch the stuff.

History repeated itself, and I married and had kids young. My husband expected me to be a homemaker. For fifteen years, I replaced my dreams with his, and supported him, all the while, feeling trapped and miserable. *I need a drink*, I thought many times. *Make it a double.* It would have been so easy to crawl into a bottle and stay there for a few decades. Alcoholism was in my blood. Instead, in fear of becoming my Mom, I rebelled against my husband.

When I was in my thirties, I went into therapy to work through the demons of having had an alcoholic mother and other issues. The therapist recommended that I establish ground rules to deal with her. The first: If Mom calls me when she's drunk, I was to say, "Don't call me when you're drunk." In the past, she'd call and ramble incoherently. I couldn't understand her and would make excuses to get off the phone, which annoyed her, and we'd wind up having an argument that wrecked me for hours. I didn't think setting guidelines would work and told the therapist, "She won't even hear me." She urged me to give it a try.

The next morning, I had my chance. Mom called at around 10 a.m. I listened to her ramble long enough to know she'd been drinking and said, "Don't call again if you've been drinking," and then I hung up and started sobbing. Ed was there and he held me as I unburdened and released years of pent up anger. Mom didn't call back. I think she was as stunned hearing the click as I had been hanging up the receiver. It must have made an impression on her. She called less often, at least.

A month later, when Mom's sixtieth birthday came around, Dad invited Betty and me and our families to have dinner to celebrate it. We all arrived with high hopes. But before the food arrived, Mom was already drunk. It was just like every restaurant meal I had growing up. Instead of sitting there, mortified, I stood and said, "You're drunk and we're leaving." I gathered up the kids, put on our coats, and left the restaurant. It was both terrifying and liberating.

I'd learned how to put my foot down during my interactions with her. But we still had yet to have a substantive conversation about her alcoholism or our relationship. It was the next major step in my re-covery as the child of an alcoholic. I had no idea how to do it, though. And then I had the perfect opportunity.

While reading the scripts for the first five episodes of *Dallas*, I saw immediately that Sue Ellen Ewing was the kind of woman who, like Mom, stayed very close to the rolling booze cart. I was going to portray an alcoholic on TV and presumably Mom would be watching. I had to say something before we started shooting.

I invited Mom over for the afternoon, sat her down at the dining room table, and put the stack of *Dallas* scripts in front of her. "I want you to read these," I said. "It's going to be tough for you. I'm playing the part of Sue Ellen. She's not you. She's over the top; this is TV. But I wanted to acknowledge what's happening and bring you into the process I'm going through as an actor."

She looked at me blankly. "How?"

"Read the scripts. And then we should talk about alcoholism." It was the first time anyone in our family had spoken that word to her face.

She stared at me and then looked down at her hands. I expected her to deny it, but she seemed resigned, like she knew the jig was up. Mom might've been waiting for thirty years for someone to say, "You're an alcoholic." Until that moment, we never had.

So she gathered up the scripts and went home to Palm Springs to read them. Later that day, she called and said, "Sue Ellen will be a tough character to play. But you can make a real impact."

"I know the subject matter very well."

Mom took it and was fairly calm about my being so direct.

All the common threads wound into a knot. Sue Ellen was a woman trapped in her marriage who drank to numb the pain of unrealized dreams, much like Mom had been trapped in a box of societal convention. By taking the part of Sue Ellen, I hoped to break out of my box and avoid becoming a sad, lonely, desperate woman, like Sue Ellen or my Mom.

So we had a long talk. It was my first honest conversation with my mother. I was thirty-seven. She was sixty. Mom and I were finally starting to get to know each other. It'd be many more years before we liked each other. But love felt possible now that we were being open.

She called me a few nights later, sober (she'd learned her lesson after repeated hang ups). We talked about the usual surface stuff, updates about the kids and sometimes about Dad. At the end of the phone call as we were wrapping up, I said, "I love you."

Just like the word "alcoholism," love wasn't spoken of in our home. I'd never said the word to either of my parents, and they'd never said them to me. It simply came out without conscious thought. Mom was stunned. She didn't respond in kind, but it didn't matter. I realized that all along, what had made me so mad at her wasn't that I didn't feel her love, but that I'd been denied the joy of loving and respecting her. It was an amazing breakthrough for me. I hung up the phone and started sobbing. I called Betty to tell her what happened.

"But will she ever get sober?" Betty asked.

"Who knows?"

My niece, Leslie, seventeen, Betty's daughter, was a member of the "talk it out" generation. Unlike us, the "sweep it under the rug" generation, Leslie felt like we had to address Marge's drinking as a family, full on. It wasn't enough to hang up on her or walk out of restaurants. It was our duty to get her sober. Leslie's first step was to send Marge an AA pamphlet. Leslie popped it into a mailbox on the Friday of Memorial Day weekend.

Ed, the kids, and I were in Aspen at our friend Merv's house. On Saturday, Betty called, hysterical. At first, I thought it was about Mom and my stomach sank. But it wasn't about Mom or Dad. Leslie, my niece, had been roller-skating across the street and was struck and killed by a stoned-out-of-her-mind driver. Merv had a private plane and brought us home to Los Angeles. Leslie was Kehly's cousin, but also her best friend. All of the cousins were close. I'd been like a second mother to Leslie, just as Betty had been to Jeff. We were all spinning.

As soon as we landed, the family drove straight to Betty's house and we cried in each other's arms. Betty sobbed, "I'll never see her graduate college. I'll never see her wedding. I'll never have grandchildren." It was agony.

After a while, Betty was able to tell me what had happened in detail. When Betty initially received a call from the police, they just told her there'd been an accident. "They said one of the girls was in the hospital and one was DOA," she told me. "But they wouldn't tell me over the phone which one it was."

She had to go to the police station to be told her daughter was dead.

Only Leslie had died. (The driver? Not a scratch.) It was like God reached down and took her. One minute she was here, a bright young thing with her whole life ahead of her. The next she was gone, nothing left but a memory. She'd been in exactly the wrong place at exactly the wrong time. It's almost like she shined too brightly to live. Leslie had the gift of bringing people together. If it was Groundhog Day, Leslie said, "Let's have a party!" Ever been to a Full Moon fiesta? I have, planned by Leslie. Talk about appreciating every moment. Leslie celebrated every day. I relied on her to play the big sister role for Kehly and Jeff. Betty and Leslie took them on camping trips and family outings when I had to work. I felt guilty about not being there, but knowing my kids were in the excellent care of my niece and sister took some of the sting out. Her death was an unspeakable loss for all of us.

We had the funeral. The next day the AA pamphlet arrived at Mom's house, with Leslie's note asking her to just read it and think about it. Seeing the note after having just been to Leslie's funeral was enough to pull Marge out of her alcoholism. She joined AA and never drank again.

She didn't go to the Betty Ford Center, which had only just opened. She did it by going to meetings and working the steps. It wasn't easy for her. As was our way, I didn't hear a lot about her progress, but I noticed changes. She slowly became a better woman.

Mom and I did get the chance to take care of our unfinished business. We were still not the best of friends, but I was the only one left to care for her at the end of her life.

She was in her eighties, living alone in Palm Springs. Dad had died years before and Mom had to learn basic life skills. She had never written a check. Dad did it all for her. I went down to Palm Springs every weekend to help her navigate practical things. Every Tuesday I took her to her doctor's appointment.

On the drive one Tuesday, she informed me that she'd started wearing Depends. "It's great! I can be anywhere and just pee," she said.

"That's fabulous, Mom," I said.

"Just pull over at the next gas station and you can put one on right now," she said. "I can give you one if you're interested."

"I'm good," I said, grinning.

In the waiting room at the doctor's office, she was greeted like a dear, beloved friend by the nurses. They thought Marge was hilarious and sweet. One of the nurses said, "Marge, would you like to come inside and get weighed?"

Mom said, "What? Would I like to get laid?"

The entire waiting room of elderly people started laughing hysterically. At eight-five, she had the lightness and silliness of a young girl, and everyone responded to it. The doctor laughed at everything she said, and I found myself giggling, too. After the appointment, we got Frappuccinos at Starbucks. She'd call me at night to ask me to remind her about basic things from her distant and recent past ("I'm out with the girls"—her crew of other eighty-plus ladies—"and I forgot what I said at the doctor's office that made everyone laugh"). She enjoyed simple pleasures: a laugh, a sugary beverage, an adult diaper. I found myself falling in love with the adorable, sweet little old lady she had become.

You have to be able to uncork pent-up anger and learn to forgive. Bottling up words, thoughts, and emotions is as prematurely aging and damaging as alcoholism. Pouring your heart out to the people you love is healing for you both. It was a healing that I'd waited for all my life. Asking Marge to read the scripts that day was the first step in our long recovery. I could have tried to do it sooner, but I don't beat myself up for not being able to. Mom and I both carried around a lot of guilt and shame about her alcoholism. We also shared the bad habit of silence. With a little help from Sue Ellen, I broke it.

IN THE DRIVER'S SEAT

For my thirty-seventh birthday, Ed bought me a butterfly pendant from Tiffany's. I collected butterfly things. The necklace was special. Besides being beautiful, it rested over my heart and reminded me of the butterfly's capacity for transformation and freedom. It was my totem.

Soon after, *Dallas* was to start filming. From the start, the *Dallas* job was logistically complicated. The producers informed the cast that we'd start filming in the city of Dallas in January—two weeks hence—and would stay until March. The actors would be put up in a motel. It was Ed's worst nightmare, what he'd expressly feared about my acting career, that one day, it would take me away from him. The kids and I hadn't been apart for even two weeks. Now we'd be separated for two months? They were at a tricky age, eleven and thirteen, when things were starting to happen for them hormonally. They needed their mother.

We had a family discussion about it. The kids said they'd be okay, but how could they comprehend how their lives would fall apart unless I was there to organize and facilitate? Ed was adamantly opposed to my leaving for "some job." He didn't order me to stay—not that that would have worked—but he campaigned hard to get me not to do the show.

With only two weeks to prepare, I threw myself into getting things done. I created a master list of a hundred items ("call the gardener," "arrange car pool," "wrap and send birthday gifts," "call the teachers"). I'd never get it all done, but in a week, I'd baked and stored sixty Crock-Pot casseroles in the freezer, including this one (it's a wonder my kids still talk to me):

Mexican Meat Pie

Ingredients

3 tsp. olive oil

1/4 cup chopped onions

1 lb. ground beef.

Taco seasoning (1 1/2 oz)

3/4 cup water

2 1/2 cans crushed tomatoes

1 1/2 cups corn kernels

2/3 cup yellow corn meal

8 corn tortillas

3 cups shredded cheddar cheese

Instructions

1. Preheat oven to 350 degrees.
2. Heat oil in a large skillet and add onions; cook until tender but not brown.
3. Add beef, brown well, and drain.
4. Mix in the taco seasoning and 3/4 cup water; let simmer for five minutes, uncovered, stirring frequently until spice mixture is no longer runny.
5. Stir crushed tomatoes, corn, and cornmeal into the meat. Mix well.
6. In a 9" round Pyrex baking dish, place four of the eight tortillas on the bottom, spread out to cover the pan.
7. Add 1/2 of the meat mixture over the tortillas.
8. Add 1/2 of the cheese.
9. Repeat the layering process until you've run out of cheese.
10. Place in oven to heat through and melt cheese (about 35 minutes).

Cut into eight pieces across like you would cut a pie!

The whirl of activity had a purpose, other than taking care of business on the eve of departure. I used it to distract myself from guilt. What kind of mother and wife would leave her family for some job? As I ran around checking things off my list ("order chicken feed," "dog food," "hire housekeeper"), I felt like a horrible, selfish monster. My friends asked, "What are you doing? You're abandoning your family." Even the head of Lorimar, *Dallas*'s production company, a friend of ours, was dead set against me doing the show. "We won't be able to take couples vacations together," he complained. Except for Betty, who was always supportive, no one in my personal life understood why I wanted to do the show. I was alone on this one.

I agonized, but there was no way I wasn't going. The universe had given me a gift. I fantasized about how much fun it was going to be. I'd hang out with this group of talented, creative people. I didn't have to cook and clean. It was going to be a glamorous escape from drudgery, like sneaking off for a mad, passionate affair.

The winter of 1978 turned out to be the coldest in Texas history. Major snow storms, freezing temperatures, wind that would peel your face off. We were shooting mainly exteriors on the porch at South-fork. My teeth chattered while I delivered my few lines. I spent much of the first week shivering in my trailer. I didn't have a lot to do. Sue Ellen was J.R.'s eye candy wife. My juiciest lines were, "More coffee, darling?" and "I have a headache." Victoria Principal and Patrick Duffy as Pam and Bobby were the heroes. Larry Hagman as J.R. was the villain. And I was the brunette on the couch with a drink in her hand.

My *Dallas* affair was a bit tepid.

I called home every night. Much to my relief and disappointment, everyone got along just fine without me. The kids arrived at school on time. They bonded with the housekeeper and ate the casseroles. Ed stepped up and was a present and responsible father. Our friends took it upon themselves to help Ed with the kids and to keep him entertained in my absence. He became a popular third wheel in Canyon Country, going from dinner to dinner. I'd worried for nothing.

It was worse for me than it was for them. I was lonely. Patrick and Larry brought their families with them to Dallas for the winter. I liked them all, and we had a few getting-to-know-you dinners. But we weren't close yet. It would have been awkward to let my hair down with them or glom onto their family time. Most nights, I hung out in my little motel room, climbing the walls with boredom. I'd never been on my own before. Until I married Ed at twenty-one, I lived with my parents. Ed and I always socialized as a couple. Girlfriend weekends or girl's night out? I'd never been. If I went to a party or club, Ed was by my side. So now I had to keep my own company. I read and watched TV while the snow piled up outside. I went a little stir-crazy.

A movie. I would go see a movie. Just taking myself out at night was a major undertaking. I didn't know the city at all. Driving around in the dark alone was scary. I got lost a couple of times and almost turned back, but I forced myself on.

Eventually I found the theater and bought a ticket. "Just one?" asked the boy in the booth. It sounded like an insult.

I bought myself a popcorn. "Just one?" asked the girl behind the counter. A theme was emerging.

The Goodbye Girl with Richard Dreyfuss and Marsha Mason was getting Oscar buzz, so I chose that. The theater was full of couples. I felt self-conscious, with good reason. I was the only single woman there. I might as well have been wearing a sign that read, A-L-O-N-E. I looked at all the pairs of heads in the seats in front of me, and imagined the people behind me looking at my head, just one, and pitying me, a woman by herself at a romantic movie, with her sad, small bag of popcorn.

"You can do this," I told myself a few times. I held on to the butterfly charm like a life preserver.

The lights went down and I focused on the story instead of my self-consciousness. At the end of the movie, the Richard Dreyfuss character, an actor, had a great job opportunity that would take him away from home and his new family for a month. The Marsha Mason character wasn't happy about it. Dreyfuss gave a great speech. I'm paraphrasing, but he said, "This is not 'some job.' It's my career. I'm doing it." It was a sign of the times that I identified with the male lead. If the gender roles had been reversed and the girlfriend ran off for "some job," I don't know if movie audiences would have applauded. Anyway, it was a nice confirmation for me. Actors go where the work is.

At the movie's end, I felt part of the audience, and not one lone woman. My anxiety about being judged evaporated. In fact, I felt elated. I'd done it. I'd gone out into the world by myself for the first time at thirty-seven, not just to the movies, but to Dallas, to a whole new world of work.

I drove home in triumph, but shared my joy with no one. It would seem like a small victory to a man, and it was just too personal to share anyway. What was the big deal? I went to the movies. I was no longer afraid of driving alone, sitting alone—of being alone. But it was more than that. I held my butterfly pendant and felt like I'd been set free.

In those early days of the show, we wore a lot of our own clothes. The butterfly charm is in the original publicity stills, and is plainly visible in nearly all of Sue Ellen's season one scenes. In a few, I worried it, like a bead.

Fiddling with my jewelry gave me something to do. Usually, the focus of the action was on the other characters. Larry and I stood in the background and bickered to ourselves as wives and their sociopathic husbands are wont to do.

In one scene, Larry improvised, "A button fell off my shirt, Wife. Fix it."

I looked at him, and thought, *Who would marry this guy? What an asshole!* My character had to have some serious self-esteem issues, and hidden courage, to stay with him. Instead of playing Sue Ellen as the docile yes-woman (my role at home), I gave her some fire.

I said, "I don't sew buttons."

Larry gaped at me, surprised by my spunk. He said, "Listen here, Wife. When I tell you to . . ." We were off and running, fully absorbed in our tiff about buttons in the background while the other actors were performing the real scene.

The director said, "Hey, what's going on over there?"

We were more interesting than the scripted bits. Before long, I got meatier lines to chew on. Scenes focused on the hate-love relationship between Sue Ellen and J.R. My credit was upgraded from "supporting" to "starring" two seasons later.

My affair with *Dallas* was heating up. Just hanging around on set was like being plugged in to the universe. My energy level soared. I clutched my butterfly like a philosopher's stone. It'd helped me turn lead into gold. As my role and confidence grew, I spent more time with Patrick, Larry, and their families and began our lifelong friendships.

There was no going back to my old life on the farm after that. In March, I returned to Canyon Country, to Ed and the kids, the animals, the house, and our friends. But I never went back into the cocoon. I was free to fly wherever I wanted.

As a shield, my butterfly protected me from slings and arrows, and the forces that tried to bring me down. But as protection against loneliness, I didn't need it. I grew to cherish my alone time as the ultimate freedom, and wished I had more of it to do whatever I wanted, when and how I liked.

When the cast was called to MGM Studios for our first day of filming in Los Angeles, I drove in and saw the giant MGM sign, the roaring lion, that I'd been looking at my whole life. As a girl, I collected autographs from the actors. That day I drove in as an actor. I had to pull over to the curb to control my emotions. A huge smile came over me as I wondered what the future held for this very grateful woman. How interesting to see how the universe works in such strange and mysterious ways.

• • •

According to a 2010 study by a British insurance company of women in twelve countries, their #2 fear about aging is Dying Alone. (FYI: #1 is losing your looks; #3 is going broke; #4 is getting cancer; #5 is being a burden on your family.) The nightmare scenario is dropping dead, no one finding the body for days, and when they do, cats have eaten it.

Why do cats *always* play the bad guy? It doesn't seem fair.

In the days of cell phones and computer cameras, it's unlikely that any of us will actually endure the nightmare scenario yet it persists in people's imaginations for another reason—beneath the fear of Dying Alone is a bigger fear, that of Living Alone.

Women are so attuned to thinking about the needs and feelings of others. Without people to respond to, some women don't know what to do with themselves. They fill every silence with chitchat and schedule every last minute of their weekends. It's like they do anything and everything to avoid being alone in their thoughts. We all know someone like this. When I'm with such people, I always wonder, why can't they relax? What are they afraid will happen if they slow down and just exist?

For peace of mind, it's essential to be able to quiet your mind and silence the constant barrage of the plugged-in world.

Yes, the California native is going to talk about meditation now.

I grew up praying, asking for favors from God, and waiting and waiting for answers. In 1973, I was introduced to meditation and was told to listen instead of asking for favors. Listen? Listen to what? To whom? Would I really hear someone speaking to me or would it simply be a subtle voice whispering in my ear? I liked the idea of asking *and* listening. My guru on the matter assured me I could do both. It sounded interesting, so I gave it a try.

I was given a mantra and instructed to silently chant and listen for twenty minutes twice a day. I got in the practice of doing it when I woke up and right before bed. As it turned out, I could listen and pray at the same time. I multitasked with the infinite and liked it. I've been meditating ever since.

Beginners can start by sitting in a chair in a quiet room, and just focusing on your breath, count inhale-exhale cycles up to ten and then start over again at one. When your mind wanders, gently bring it back to the breath. If you can last two minutes, great! Gradually increase up to twenty minutes. The practice protects you from stress, lowers your blood pressure, and grounds you for the hectic day ahead. And if you get really good at it, you can get a preview of what's to come.

As Maya Angelou said, "Listen to yourself and in that quietude you might hear the voice of God."

PULL THE TRIGGER

In the early days of *Dallas*, I set about getting to know Sue Ellen Ewing from the inside out. I understood her need to drink and I got the loveless marriage part. But who was she? Where did she come form? What did she do when she wasn't drinking or having affairs? I needed to flesh out the character to make her come alive.

Before we started filming, I tagged along with Ed to a photo shoot with Dolly Parton, Linda Ronstadt, and Emmylou Harris. While he was setting up, I sat with Dolly and told her that I had just been cast in a series set in Texas, but I wasn't so sure about my accent. Dolly said, "Oh, honey, just talk like me!" Every word out of her mouth dripped sugar.

But it didn't sound Texan. "Where are you from?" I asked.

"Georgia!"

"Yeah, well, you're about a thousand miles off!"

I began to research the phonetics of the Texan accent and eventually hired Hollywood dialect coach Robert Easton to be my personal Henry Higgins. Robert was the ultimate expert. If you talked to him for five minutes, he could tell you what street you grew up on. Physically, he was an impressive fellow, a barrel-chested curmudgeon with white hair and a goatee, like an intellectual Colonel Sanders. We worked and worked on it, rounding vowels into a tape recorder, putting candy in my mouth and making me repeat, "The rain on the plains of Texas hardly ever happens" (maybe that was a scene from *My Fair Lady* or I just dreamed it). Anyway, he helped my accent evolve from too sing-songy and weird to the subtle sounds of Sue Ellen.

Since I didn't get a lot of lines at first, my initial bad accent wasn't that obvious. As a background player, I had the luxury of developing my character as I went along. I made a habit of going to the Neiman Marcus Northpark Mall and studying the rich Dallas wives in their natural environment. How did they dress, walk, eat, talk? What clothes did they wear and what bags did they carry? These ladies would regularly drop thousands in an hour without batting a false eyelash. Money was no object to them, and it couldn't be to Sue Ellen.

I went to upscale salons to observe the ladies. I overheard one woman tell her friend, "I've got to run. I have to go fluff and fold for my sweetheart before he gets home." I asked the salon owner later why that woman had to run home and do her laundry, and learned that the expression "fluff and fold" in Dallas meant to primp oneself. It was the practice of certain Dallas wives to have full hair and makeup and to dress to the nines for their husbands when they came home from work. Even if Sue Ellen hated J.R., it would be a point of pride to always look her best.

Another night I went to a party at the Mansion, a very elegant hotel. I was in the ladies' room at the mirror, putting on lipstick, when a beautiful Southern lady joined me at the mirror. She opened her Judith Leiber purse. Inside was a lipstick and a gun. I said, "Excuse me. Is that a real gun?"

She looked at me like I was from Mars. "Of course, darlin'. This is Texas!"

My education in Sue Ellen had taken me to a strange place, with odd customs. You had to be coiffed, bejeweled, fluffed, folded, and packing heat at all times. I learned the makeup, the mannerisms, the language, the attitude. Slowly, my character evolved, and became real to me, and to our fans. I always tell young actors to do their homework. If you research the character, it's so much easier and more fulfilling to play the part. I see it as loading up a red wagon full of treasures to bring to the party. Don't show up empty-handed or you'll feel like an idiot.

By the third season of *Dallas*, I had Sue Ellen down. We'd all settled into our characters and the show was really taking off. None of us had any idea just how big it would get.

During the summer of 1980, Dallas was red hot. A deadly heat wave melted Dallas/Fort Worth with sixty-nine days of temperatures over 100 degrees. In June we had three consecutive days at 113 degrees. You might think Texas is just as infernal every summer. Not true! The summer of 1980 shattered records and held on to the hellish glory for another thirty-one years until 2011. The record high of 113 degrees set June 26 to 28, 1980, stands as Dallas/Fort Worth's hottest days in recorded history.

Also that June, comedian Richard Pryor set himself on fire freebasing cocaine. Ronald Reagan was running a scorched-earth campaign against incumbent Jimmy Carter. Tempers flared all over the world, including Iraq, where the new leader, Saddam Hussein, refused to sign peace treaties with neighboring countries. The hostages in Iran had been held for over a year by then and the yellow ribbons around trees at home wilted in the heat. The Cold War was heating up, too, with both the U.S. and the USSR testing nuclear weapons.

With all this madness in the news, the number one topic of conversations around dinner tables, backyard barbecues, and air-conditioned cafés that summer began with the question, "Who shot J.R.?"

That phrase was on bumper stickers, T-shirts, posters. During the election, Republican campaigners gave out buttons that read, A DEMOCRAT SHOT J.R. Jimmy Carter tried to get in on the conversation. At a fund-raiser in Texas, he told his supporters, "I came to Dallas to find out confidentially who shot J.R. If any of you could let me know that, I could finance the whole campaign this fall." The shooting was parodied on *Saturday Night Live*. Pop novelty songs were written about it. Odds makers in Las Vegas took millions in bets on who pulled the trigger. Sue Ellen was considered a long shot at twenty-five to one.

The fan frenzy spread around the world. Half the population of Britain watched J.R. take a couple of bullets to the chest. While Larry Hagman was touring London that summer, the Queen Mother of England asked him, "Would you care for some tea? Quite. Lovely. Indeed. Now, if you please, who shot you?" Or something to that affect. He said, "Not even for you, Your Majesty."

By the time the "Who Done It?" episode aired in November, our show had become a global phenomenon that hasn't been repeated in the thirty-five years since. In the United States, eighty million people watched the episode, more than had voted in the presidential election a few weeks before. It was the highest rated show in history and remains the second most viewed episode of all time, topped only by the M*A*S*H series finale. The worldwide audience for "Who Done It?" topped 370 million people in fifty-seven countries.

Dallas was red-hot that summer, too, and I was in the middle of it. The producers and writers were praised for inventing the cliff-hanger season finale (commonplace today). The truth is, they were at a loss for how to end the season, so they said, "Screw it, let's just shoot someone." They made the smart decision to shoot Larry and wrapped for the season without any idea who they were going to pin it on, or even whether J.R. would survive. (Larry was negotiating his contract.) They couldn't possibly have known how the world would react.

I'm not a social anthropologist, so I don't speak with authority on why fans went nuts over a fake crime on a TV show that had no resemblance to real life. My theory is that people liked having something silly to talk about instead of the hostages, the gas crisis, double-digit mortgage rates, the Cold War, the election, and nuclear testing. Also, because of the masculine energy on the show, with Larry and Patrick leading the pack, men felt comfortable joining the national conversation about what was really just a soap opera. Speculating about the culprit at the water cooler was not just socially acceptable. It was an imperative. *Dallas* was rare common ground among genders, classes, races, and religions.

The tension was heightened because of a writers strike in Hollywood. There were no new episodes of our—or any—TV show for months. We filmed the shooting in March and the big reveal didn't air until November, eight months later. (I'm not going to call it a spoiler alert, just a gentle reminder: The shooter was J.R.'s duplicitous and curvaceous sister-in-law, Kristin Shepard, played by Mary Crosby.) It was an interminable length of time for the audience to wait, but the fans endured the mystery together. Instead of fading, anticipation grew.

During our hiatus, I was back at home on our farm, being a wife and mom, feeding the chickens. I got a taste of what was happening when I went to the supermarket. I pushed my cart down the aisle and every few feet, someone would say, "Hey, Sue Ellen! Who shot J.R.?" I went to the next aisle and it would happen again. When we went to Hawaii for our family vacation that summer, fans kept coming to our table at lunch, asking for autographs and photos. The kids were so annoyed. This was our time together and we were constantly interrupted. I tried to be nice. Some people agreed to let us finish our meal, but some refused to leave the table.

It was before the age of paparazzi jumping out of the bushes. I don't know how anyone can handle that. I was not prepared for the amount of attention we got, not by a long shot. In only a few years, I went from being a thirty-eight-year-old housewife to world famous. When I started acting, I assumed I'd get recognized. But who could have expected fame of that order? There wasn't a class at UCLA to audit called "How to Handle Fame." (There probably is now.)

As many celebrities have said, there's an upside and a downside to fame. Both are fairly predictable. Part of being famous was fun. Part was baffling. I was surprised that people kept asking me what I had for breakfast. Part was terrifying. Larry and I went on a promotional tour in France that year. We appeared on a talk show and when we left the studio, we walked out to our car in the alley. We had to push through the crowd to get to it. Once we were inside, fans swarmed the car and started rocking it. They were jumping on the roof and pushing their faces against the glass, screaming, "J.R.! Sue Ellen!" The driver couldn't move. I burst into tears, thinking, *This is how I'm going to die. Crushed to death in an alley in France.*

I'm not complaining about anything that happened. I bless it. Fame opened the door to a lifetime as a professional actor. For me, it was always about the work. Getting up and going to the set. Playing a part and acting through an emotionally fraught scene. I loved everything about the work. Fame eclipsed it. It cast a long shadow on my creativity. In fact, my most creative years came *after* the heyday of my fame.

It's true for anyone, in any profession. When the ambition of youth is gone, when you're not driven by money, ego, vanity, one-upmanship, rivalries, competitiveness, having something to prove, all you're left with is the crystal joy of creativity that attracted you to your chosen career in the first place. Thanks to *Dallas*, I'm still acting on stage and on TV. But if I were doing it in a shoe box, I'd be okay.

I mentioned all the way back in the book's introduction that these are our Wisdom Years, they are our Wonder Years, too, when you can step out of the shadow of whatever eclipsed your creativity for whatever reason way back when. Write that novel. Learn piano. Audition for a community theater play. Not only will it give you a twinkle in the eye, creatively stimulating the brain wards off dementia, especially playing music.

I was lucky enough to see a recent revival of Kaufman and Hart's *You Can't Take It With You*, and found myself furiously nodding along at Grandpa Vanderhof's last big speech to convince Mr. Kirby, a stuck-up Wall Streeter, to let his son Tony pursue his heart's desire, or else wind up as miserable as his father for abandoning his own youthful dreams.

"How many of us would be willing to settle when we're young for what we eventually get?" he asked. "All those plans we made . . . what happened to them? It's only a handful of the lucky ones who can say they even came close."

Here's the thing: It's never too late to take your shot. Hurry up and pull that trigger. Should you miss the mark, who cares? Re-aim. Take another shot. If anyone questions you, just tell them, "Kristin did it."

THE BIGGER THE HAIR, THE CLOSER TO GOD

In 1977 my hair was the suburban Mom version of a Suzi Quatro shag. Blah length, blah bangs, blah brown. Karlys Daly would have been appalled. I couldn't very well play a pampered, wealthy Texan with Housewife Head. I needed a look. Something had to be done, and fast.

Victoria Principal suggested I see her stylist, José Eber. I'd heard of him, of course. I lived on a farm, not under rock. He'd famously created the icon styles of the day, from Farrah Fawcett's tousled lioness look to Katherine Ross's sexy wave to Goldie Hawn's soft layers. Victoria helped me get an appointment. We'd shifted production from Dallas to our regular home in Culver City at Lorimar Studios where we shot most of the scenes on a soundstage. It was only too easy for me to go to José's salon in Beverly Hills one afternoon.

The first thing he said to me was, "You're so much younger in person." My current style was aging me. Not good. He suggested a three-step overhaul. First he'd give me a permanent wave. Next he would lighten my dark brown by three shades. Last, he'd cut loads of layers and side-swept fringe. The man mussed the heads of Cher and Barbara Walters. I figured I could trust him.

José is French and to this day, wears a cowboy hat with a long braid. He has an aristocratic aura. In another life he might have been Marie Antoinette. In this life, he is a magician. Instead of a wand he uses scissors. Snipping here and there, he gave me a sassy, sexy cut that changed my face, how I felt about myself, and how people treated me. I walked in a frump and strutted out feeling like a star. It was the beginning of a beautiful friendship. He was in charge of my head for the entire first run of *Dallas*. I was honored to be included in his 1982 best seller *Shake Your Head, Darling*, along with an impressive roster of A-listers of the era.

The following year, I told José that I was frustrated shooting scenes outside the Southfork Ranch in a strong wind. My hair whipped in my face and got stuck in my lip gloss. I had to resort to pinning it back with a butterfly clip. It looked cheap, not elegant, and Sue Ellen should always be elegant, even when she was chugging vodka in a tornado.

He said, "Letz do somezing differante." He snipped a bit in the back, a bit on the sides, and gave me shorter layers on top. *Et voilà*, La Mullet a la José was born. I returned to the set to start filming the second half of the season, all excited to show off my new rockin' do—so rockin' I looked a bit like Rod Stewart or David Bowie in his *Diamond Dogs* period. The producers took one look at me and went ballistic. They mimed slashing their wrists and hanging themselves. It wasn't that bad! The problem was continuity. My hair would be completely different in one scene to the next. I hadn't realized there was a clause in my contract that forbid changing my appearance without approval.

"The explanation is that Sue Ellen went to the salon between scenes and got a haircut," I said helpfully.

"You look like a lesbian," said the producer.

Looking at old photos of that cut, I think his comment was an insult to lesbians. But the style quickly caught on and became that year's hot look. I actually won a place on a few magazine Best Tressed lists in 1979. It must have been the Year of the Rooster.

A woman can't rest on her mullets. José had big plans for my hair as we rolled into a new decade. After I grew it for a while, José and I reached skyscraper glam-rock heights. In the 1980s, the deeply held belief was that the bigger the hair, the closer you were to God. Mine was knocking on heaven's door.

I was nominated for an Emmy Award in 1981 for Best Lead Actress in a Dramatic Series. It was a major honor and I was thrilled. José and I talked about what we'd do for the big night. We agreed that my hair had to make a larger-than-life statement. High impact. So he broke out *two* cans of VO5. José teased my hair into a fluffy, puffy confection, down and very curly.

The plan was that I'd go to the salon in the afternoon. José would do his magic and his staff would tackle everything else (skin, nails, makeup). Ed would pick me up in a limo on the way to the awards dinner. I had my outfit with me at José's: a short, black, backless halter dress. My curly poodle hair fit the fun, flirty vibe of the dress perfectly.

Before a final misting, José said, "Shake your head, darling!"

I did, and was dizzy with excitement. With my high hair and slip of a dress, I looked as fun and pretty as I felt.

Ed arrived in the limo and came into the salon in his tux. José introduced me, and I made a grand entrance into the room. I did a lap around the salon—"I'm walking here!"—for Ed, and it felt like I was seventeen again back in Saul Rubenstein's showroom. I might've done a Stevie Nicks twirl.

Ed said, "You look like a hooker."

José's face collapsed. I think I stammered an apology for my rude husband, and then Ed and I left. We sat in the back seat of the limo together, not touching, not talking. The network put a bottle of champagne in the car. We didn't open it.

Usually, Ed hid his criticism in a joke. *You look like a hooker, bah-dum-bum*—CHING! But there wasn't a trace of humor in his voice.

It was the biggest night of my life, and in a roomful of people who'd worked hard on my appearance, Ed said I looked like a prostitute. I was crushed. I found it hard to breathe and needed air, but I didn't dare open the windows and mess my hair.

My theory was that Ed wanted to take me down a peg. He'd forbidden me to take acting classes. He had urged me to quit *Dallas*. Now I was up for a major award, and I'd done it all on my own. He equated my success with defiance.

Back then, the Emmy Awards were a formal dinner. Ed and I found our table. I sat next to Loni Anderson who was nominated in comedy for *WKRP*. We both lost. We commiserated and tried to cheer each other up. Ed's mood improved considerably after I lost.

It really was an honor to be nominated. Losing was a disappointment, but it paled in comparison to how livid and hurt I was about Ed's behavior that night. He was a famous art director—still is, posthumously. He was well respected and made plenty of money. Yet he was so resentful and threatened by my success he had to tear me down to elevate himself. But I held my head up high. I held my hair up even higher.

I'd fantasized about leaving my marriage before, but I'd never considered it a serious option until that night. How could I stay married to someone who was rooting for me to fail? It wasn't healthy for either of us—or our children—to live with so much bitterness and jealousy on his part, and resentment and disappointment on mine.

There's a photo of our arrival at the event that night. We'd just stepped out of the limo and paused for some photographers. We stood together and beamed. Ed's hand was wrapped around my arm possessively. We seemed excited to be there, a happy couple celebrating together. I should have won the Emmy for that moment alone.

When I look at the photo, though, I don't fixate on Ed's hand or my fake smile. All I see is a great dress and shiny, bouncy hair.

I looked pretty.

It's been thirty-six years since that night, and Ed's behavior is forgiven if not forgotten. I sympathize with what he was going through.

He took one look at me at José's salon that night and he must have known he was losing me. He was hurt, and he hurt me in return. Our marriage, like a bad haircut, had to be grown out.

Our perspective changes almost as frequently and dramatically as hairstyles over the years. Painful memories, like bad haircuts, become things we shake our heads about, darling. The joyful memories get bigger and closer to God.

GOING GRAY HAIR RULES

First, some suggestions from the professional. José mentioned the spirit of these rules about hair and age in *Shake Your Head, Darling*:

STYLE IS AN ATTITUDE, NOT A NUMBER. If you get a grannie gray helmet, you'll transmit your chronological age to everyone you meet. Not that you should get a very young style, either. Strike that balance between age-appropriate and aging. You're only as old as your haircut.

LONG HAIR ON OLDER WOMEN IS OKAY IF YOU HAVE THE ATTITUDE TO PULL IT OFF. For some, long hair is a curtain to hide behind. If that's true, I'd say cut it off. If you just adore long hair and flaunt it proudly, keep it.

THINK SOFT. Severe styles can seem extreme on a softer, older face. Light layers are more flattering for the over-sixty crowd.

As for my suggestions, the main one is to pay attention to how you feel. Do you look at yourself in the mirror and say, "I look *gooood*"? Wonderful. If you look in the mirror and think, *BLAHH* or *BLECCH*, that's not healthy for the soul. Hair is the easiest aspect of our appearance to change. All you have to do is call the José in your life and get a mullet.

Kidding. Don't get a mullet.

Here are my thoughts on hair based on observations of friends, other actors, public figures, and my own experience:

BANGS ARE BEAUTIFUL. When I noticed some forehead wrinkles, I got long, layered bangs to cover them. I mentioned it to my friend Valerie Harper, and she went out that day and got bangs, too. I think we both look pretty good.

IF YOUR HAIR DOESN'T MOVE IN THE WIND, YOU'RE USING TOO MUCH PRODUCT. If you're using a lot of product because you need extra volume, there is no shame in getting permanent extensions or using clip-ons. Ask your stylist to show you how they work.

WIGS ARE YOUR FRIEND. As an actor, I'm comfortable wearing wigs on occasion. If your hair is thinning with age or the texture has turned to wire, wigs are a great option. Quality wigs are made with human hair, in all kinds of styles (they're not all country music star hair). Just explore and educate yourself about what's out there.

GO LIGHTER. Or go gray! Why not? Men do it and they look great. My gray isn't silvery delicious, so I veer from strawberry blond to light brown. Dark hair on older skin looks a bit harsh. Even adding highlights can make a world of difference.

SHAGS AND CHIN-LENGTH BOBS ARE UNIVERSALLY FLATTERING. Especially true for older woman. Look at Jane Fonda, Helen Mirren, and Diane Keaton.

PIXIE CUTS ARE HIGH MAINTENANCE, BUT SENSATIONAL. If you can get to the salon once a month, a well-managed pixie like Judi Dench's is sexy and cool. A confident pixie walks in the room and everyone turns and says, "Who's *that?*"

BE PRACTICAL. Your hair, like your life, is unique. Your hairstyle has to fit in to your lifestyle. Don't get a high-maintenance look if you know from experience that you just don't have the time or inclination to keep up with it. If you find that you're always just pulling it back into a ponytail, then your style is too much for you. I'm not saying don't get the style of your dreams. Just remember that you're going to be awake with it, too.

DON'T BE A MUTTON SHORN LIKE A LAMB. Have you changed your look recently? Break out the photo books. If your hair is the same color and cut as it was twenty years ago, it's time for a change. Not only will a new style be more appropriate for the changes in your face and hair texture, you won't look like you're trying to pull off a too young look. I know women who've worn the same style for decades because of inertia. Others feel guilty spending money on a style that needs a lot of maintenance. It does add up. But I think of getting your hair done regularly as a little something you do for yourself that can make a huge impact on your day-to-day life.

My Hair Mask Recipe

Every month or so, I give myself a hair mask treatment of my own design.

½ avocado

1 tbsp. olive oil

½ banana

1 egg yolk

Whip all of the ingredients in a bowl until they form a batter. Massage the mixture into the hair and cover with a shower cap. Use a hair dryer to heat the shower cap once it's on your head (it makes things heat up faster). Let it sit for an hour or however long you have. Rinse using your favorite shampoo. For longer hair use a whole avocado and banana.

GONG BONG

My life had a routine. I'd get up at 4:30 a.m. and drive to Lorimar Studios in Culver City to work on *Dallas*. Then I'd go home, help the kids with their homework, study my lines for the next day, and then go off to bed I'd go. The kids loved to tell me to go to bed! They thought it was hysterical to turn the tables on me. Ed went to work, came home, and then disappeared into the guesthouse by the pool he'd converted into an art studio. This was our marriage.

I still cooked and cleaned, etc. On the *Dallas* set, I complained about the demands of being a working parent. Larry said, "What's so hard about it?" Easy for him to say—he had a traditional marriage. While he worked, his wife ran the house and raised the kids. Maj Hagman was supportive and thrilled for her husband's success. The breadwinner spouse had a reliable source of income. He enjoyed his work and came home in a good mood.

I came home exhausted. I had a hired housekeeper, but I was responsible for a million other parenting and household duties, along with working twelve-hour days on the show. My marriage was exhausting, too. It had been over for years already. But neither one of us made a move to physically leave.

That song, "Should I Stay or Should I Go?" by the Clash came out in 1982, during the height of my marital Cold War. The kids, fifteen and seventeen, played it nonstop on the boombox. It seemed to be everywhere: in the supermarket, in elevators, on the car radio. I couldn't escape that song and its burning question.

REASONS TO STAY

It's not so easy to end a twenty-two-year marriage. We shared property, children, friends, and a history. Our lives were interwoven and would require fine tweezers to tease apart, painfully.

The kids were at the age when the focus should be on them and their future. Jeff was about to apply to colleges and Kehly was a hormonal mess. They didn't need a major disruption in their home life.

Celebrity divorces weren't treated with kid gloves by the media. How would the news of my divorce play out on the front page of tabloids? I didn't want to find out.

Divorce was a big deal in any case. Nowadays, marriages are swapped out like winter and summer wardrobes. Back then, divorce was seen as a personal failure and the wife, nine times out of ten, was to blame. Audiences were shocked by the 1978 movie *An Unmarried Woman* with Jill Clayburgh, which showed a jilted wife getting on with her life, having sex and being happy as a single woman. It was considered revolutionary.

No one in my family had been divorced, going back as far as anyone could remember. Previous generations suffered in silence through their bad marriages rather than face failure and disgrace.

I'd adapted to how things were. It wasn't horrible. I didn't have a reason to end it, like if he beat me, did drugs, or cheated. There was no event that I could point to and say, "That's why I left."

REASONS TO GO

Only one item in this category: I was miserable.

I thought, *If I don't get out of this marriage, I will die.*

I went back and forth for months. Betty was my confidante and we talked about everything. Her marriage had been rocked by Leslie's death, and we spent many hours discussing our problems. Betty also understood how private a person I was. I was afraid to stay in a marriage that was suffocating and not supportive, but I was terrified to leave and go through a divorce in the public eye. Betty counseled me wisely. "Life is short," she said. "When you can't stand it for one more day, you'll be able to go."

And that's what happened. It was as if a tidal wave had been rising up above me for years. When finally it came crashing down over me, I knew I couldn't stay even for one more day. It was undeniable. I had to go. Now.

Once I made the decision to leave, I couldn't get out of there fast enough. On the sly, I quietly started looking at houses in Malibu with a realtor. I rented a furnished place on the beach—only a mile from Larry and Maj's. I didn't tell anyone. The rental contract signed, I went home, packed a duffle bag of clothes and a toothbrush.

When Ed came home, I told him, "I can't be married anymore." My voice broke. I was weary, beaten down, overwhelmed, just raw, raw, raw.

He barely reacted. "Okay," he said. "Do what you have to do." I think he was in denial. His words had the usual tinge of condescension, like he was indulging his wacky wife in her little escapade. He assumed I'd come home with my tail between my legs.

We brought the kids into our bedroom. They sat on the bed. Ed and I stood in front of them. I said, "Kids, I'm so sorry. Your father and I are going to separate. It's got nothing to do with you. It's between Dad and me. We love you. I'll always be your mom, but right now I can't be married and I'm moving out."

Like their father, the kids didn't react much. Their deeper emotions didn't surface until later.

I hugged and kissed them good-bye and said I'd call later, and then I drove straight to the beach. It was a dark and stormy night (really). I sank into the couch, watched the rain on the water, and thought, *What have I done?*

My private decision didn't stay that way for long. The realtor ratted me out. He gave an interview to the *National Enquirer*, saying that I'd rented a house in Malibu and had abandoned my loving and supportive husband and my kids. I hadn't breathed a word to the realtor about my personal life.

After the news broke, our mutual friends wanted nothing to do with me. Just like in *An Unmarried Woman*, our couple friends took Ed's side. He'd had all those third-wheel dinners. He didn't pose a threat to their marriages. But I was suddenly a single woman, a celebrity with her own money. The neighborhood wives treated me like Ebola. Not one called to see how I was holding up or asked to meet for a drink. They were too busy cooking casseroles and visiting Ed, like he'd been stricken with a fatal disease and needed round-the-clock care. I didn't see or talk to any of those women again. I did hear from many of their husbands, who kindly offered to come to my house in Malibu to give me a shoulder to cry on. I was horrified at the thought.

I was in Malibu for several days before Ed showed up. He was getting nervous now, like I might actually be serious. We sat on the couch that faced the ocean. I said, "I was suffocating. I got no support from you when I needed it most."

"I have supported you," he said.

In his mind, he had been supportive because he tolerated my shooting schedule. But the truth was, he hated my success. At first I was the awestruck cheerleader for him, the model bride who was so impressed with him and did whatever he asked. But when the tables turned and I stopped being his cheerleader, started rooting for myself and asked him to be supportive of me, he was hostile and resentful.

I said, "I don't agree."

"Where is this coming from? We never fight."

True. We didn't yell. But we weren't caring, sharing partners either. It was more like living with a roommate who gave me no emotional support, but was critical and judgmental.

In the end, I just didn't like myself with Ed. When we're in relationships with others, we get a chance to view ourselves through their eyes. I didn't like what I saw of myself in Ed's eyes. He was my husband for a reason and he was one of my greatest teachers. If not for our marriage, our two beautiful children wouldn't have been born. Our marriage allowed me to observe the compromises necessary for a marriage to function. If I hadn't felt crushed by those compromises, I wouldn't have excavated deeply into the Rabbit Hole to learn about the universe, the soul, and myself. Ed was to be honored for following his path, his dreams, for being a great father and the best husband he knew how to be. He did his best, as we all do.

But his best wasn't enough for me.

The conversation went round and round. I'm not sure he understood why I did what I did, but I tried to explain myself. When he left, I remember feeling waves of relief. On the crest of that, though, the guilt. The kids, like Ed, understood by now that I was serious. Jeff reacted with his usual mysterious silence, but I knew there was chaos underneath. Kehly acted happy about the separation. Now she had a house in the country and a house on the beach. It was her honeymoon period with our divorce. I knew it wasn't real. This was a major upheaval during a fragile time of her life. The reality was sure to come crashing down soon enough.

The first week, I holed up in the rental, afraid of being spotted and besieged by photographers. I was furious at the realtor and guilt ridden about the kids. I would have hidden in the house forever if I could have. Betty called to check in, but I didn't even want to see her. Several days into my self-imposed exile, there was a knock at the door. I figured I'd been found by paparazzi. I peeked out from behind a curtain.

There stood my new neighbor, friend, and "husband," Larry Hagman.

I opened the door, sobbing. He looked so sweet, holding a bottle of champagne, standing next to a Vespa scooter, wearing a tweed jacket, ascot, corduroy trousers, and an English cap. He gave me the bubbly. Then he reached in his pocket and took out a plastic bear full of soap you squeeze to make bubbles. His care package had a theme. I stood there, watching in awe, as he stood in my doorway, in his fancy pants blowing bubbles to cheer me up.

Naturally, I sobbed even harder.

We put the champagne in the fridge and then Larry said, "I'm going to introduce you to everyone in Malibu." I got on the scooter and we putted around the neighborhood for hours. Larry gave me the grand tour. I met the dry cleaner, the wine guy, the owner of the pizza place, and the green grocer. He got me laughing and eating and having fun. I was so grateful to Larry. He didn't try to get me to talk about what was happening. Larry knew he couldn't fix my marriage or mend my heart, but he could make sure I went to the right mechanic.

Larry had a tradition. Every night at sundown, he and Maj would go out on their deck and open a bottle of champagne. As the sun touched the horizon, Larry would say, "Gong! Bong!" I don't know why he did this, but it was his thing. He celebrated the passing of each and every day, and shared the moment with his wife, his kids, and whomever else was around.

That night, after our scooter tour of Malibu, Maj grilled steaks for us. When the time came, we toasted the sunset, and chanted, "Gong! Bong!" I started crying *again*. I was an open faucet during that horrible week. Larry and Maj wrapped me up in their arms. It was so nourishing, so loving. These people cared about me. I had friends. Someone was on my side.

When I first showed up at Charles Conrad's acting class, I couldn't have imagined that in less than five years, I'd become famous, would leave my husband, that my best friend would be Major Nelson from *I*

Dream of Jeannie, that we'd drink champagne on his deck, and that I'd cry until I laughed so hard, champagne came out of my nose.

When I think of how my life unfurled after my divorce I am reminded of an Anaïs Nin quote, "And the day came when the risk to remain tight in a bud was more painful than the risk it took to blossom." For years I focused on what I should do instead of following through. I leaned toward the divorce without being brave enough, secure enough, sure enough to go through with it. But when I actually took the risk, my life became my own and I was happier than I'd ever been. In the years since, I can't tell you how many women have come up to me and told me how Sue Ellen inspired them to leave unhappy marriages and how their lives bloomed open afterwards. Women need to stop obsessing about what they *should* do, and move forward. I've been thinking about the word "should" and how it goes against being at peace with yourself and your life. So, as is my wont, I made some lists:

REASONS *NOT* TO USE SHOULD

It causes inertia. "Should I?" is tacit permission to blow something off. If you give yourself the option of being lazy, you'll take it.

It fostered guilt. "I should really lose weight" or "I should get some exercise" is a constant reminder that you're not doing it.

It erodes self-esteem. "I should stop smoking," or "I should make new friends" only calls attention to the fact that you feel helpless to combat an addiction or improve your social life.

It reinforces the thing you "shouldn't" do. If you say, "I shouldn't nag my kids," your subconscious only hears "nag my kids."

It's annoying. How do you react when someone says to you, "You really should go to this restaurant?" It's like they know more than you do and are rubbing it in your face (or maybe that's how it feels on a bad day). No one likes being told what to do.

It's sabotage. As soon as I say "should," I can feel my resolve weaken. But when I use positive language, like "I choose happiness and health," there's no issue about whether or not to take my gratitude walk or make my smoothie. There's no "should" about taking care of myself. I don't say, "I should really go to bed early tonight." I just go to bed early! By removing "should," you can get so much more done. That's good. We've got so much more to do.

REASONS TO USE SHOULD

I've got nothing.

LAUGH UNTIL CHAMPAGNE
COMES OUT OF YOUR NOSE

Some of my favorite *Dallas* scenes (all searchable on YouTube):

SUE ELLEN HITS ROCK BOTTOM. This took place toward the end of my run. Sue Ellen and J.R. had a fight. Wearing hat-to-heel Valentino, Sue Ellen went on an epic bender. Drunk and disoriented (or as the English say, "tired and emotional"), she stumbled along Skid Row and was harassed by a couple of pimps (one played by a very young Lou Diamond Phillips) and a pair of strung out whores (one played by a very young Cameron Diaz; just kidding, but wouldn't that have been fabulous?). After passing out in an alley, Sue Ellen was revived by a filthy crone and asked, "Can you tell me where I am?" The crone said, "The bottom of the bottle, sweetie. Just like me." She offered Sue Ellen a drink from a green bottle in a brown bag. Sue Ellen guzzled the booze like sweet mother's milk. We had a ball in that alley. I loved it when Sue Ellen sleazed it up. When she was sober, hair and makeup took two hours. When she was wasted, it was twenty minutes. I never had more fun at work than when I played a degenerate. The only downside was my poor Valentino shirt. It got ripped when I rolled around on the street. We had to buy a back up.

SUE ELLEN SINGS THE BLUES. This scene took place at the very beginning of my run. Southfork was invaded by two crooks, one a young Brian Dennehy. He had some cockamamy reason for hating the Ewings, and sought his revenge. He forced Sue Ellen to put on a swimsuit and her Miss Texas pageant sash. She put a trench coat on over it. Then, at gunpoint, in front of the entire Ewing clan, he forced her to reenact the talent part of the competition. Through tears, Sue Ellen started warbling, "People. People who need people . . ." Dennehy yelled, "The coat!" While peeling off her trench, Sue Ellen sobbed and sang, "Are the luckiest people in the worldddd . . ." Spliced in were reaction shots of the cast as they watched. It was my musical debut, and I am no singer. Barbara Bel Geddes was checked into the hospital after that day of shooting. My singing might have put her there. It was Sue Ellen's first big moment. I wore my butterfly charm to protect me. I got through it, and learned what I was capable of as an actor. If I could stand in front of the cast in a bathing suit, singing "People" with a gun to my head, I could do anything. Any acting opportunity to be exposed, to go raw, was a breakthrough.

J.R. COMMITS SUE ELLEN TO A SANITARIUM. This came at the end of season two. Sue Ellen, a hopeless drunk, was pregnant with someone's baby (could have been any male over eighteen in all of Texas). To protect his presumed son, J.R. checked Sue Ellen into a sanitarium to dry out. As hugely pregnant Sue Ellen was dragged away by orderlies, begging for release, J.R. said, "You take care now!" Larry always said this was his favorite episode, just a crystal-clear example of how despicable J.R. was.

SUE ELLEN AND J.R. FIGHT. Of course, we fought in nearly every episode. It's like saying your favorite Gilligan's Island was when the castaways almost got off the island, but then Gilligan screwed it up.

As Sue Ellen and J.R., we fought. We threw slaps and drinks. I kneed him in the groin once, a very carefully choreographed scene. We had angry sex once on a bench press in the Southfork home gym. We threatened each other, sneered, spat, lied, screamed, and schemed. Ninety percent of my scenes on the show were with Larry, and I loved making every one of them. Whenever the cameras weren't rolling, we giggled like kids.

Larry said I was his favorite leading lady (don't tell Barbara Eden!). I've worked with some incredibly sexy leading men. But Larry will always be my favorite.

We were so comfortable with each other, people have assumed there was more between us than friendship. Nope. There was nothing romantic or sexual between us. (Sorry.) That would have been like screwing my brother. He assumed the role of my overprotective father, never approving of anyone I dated. No one was good enough for me. His wife Maj was Swedish and strong as an ox and could put up with Larry and his nonstop partying (drinking, smoking, dropping acid with rock stars). The three of us traveled together and I was like the teenage daughter who got dragged along (though not at all grudgingly). What audiences responded to on TV was a genuine connection, the magic of true friendship.

Larry was pure energy. He was a circus. After being asleep for the first thirty-eight years of my life, I was finally invited into the big tent and Larry was the ringmaster.

My life hadn't been playful until then. I'd been cooking and cleaning since I was nine. I'd worked jobs starting at sixteen and then went right into a marriage that was all work, very little joy. I didn't get the concept: What is this thing you call fun? Then all of a sudden, the lights went on. The music turned up. The circus started, and Larry was waving me in. I'd never moved so fast in my life.

The most important advice yet about getting farther along the road to happiness: Go to the circus. Play in the sandbox. Laugh until champagne comes out of your nose.

Life begins!

Betty and me right before my polio diagnosis, 1945.

Betty between Mom and Dad (look at those lapels!).
I'm to the left in the matching outfits, made by Mom, 1947.

School dance with the
shortest boy in the room, 1953.

My wedding day, 1962.

Treasured moments with
Jeff on the beach, 1965.

Christmas card, 1881.

I rode this horse in a Noxema ad, 1970.

So stiff! Career girl on the go! Models of today will be on the floor laughing, 196[...]

Mod was in at that time.

LINDA GRAY
HEIGHT/5' 8"
HAIR/BROWN
EYES/HAZEL
S.A.G.
PACIFIC ARTISTS
MARY WEBB DAVIS
8743 SUNSET BLVD.
LOS ANGELES, CALIF. 90069
657-8990

I loved working with Harry Langdon all during the '80s.

Directing my first episode, 1986.

Side bangs, care of Jose Eber, 1979.

Emmy night, 1981.
"You look like a hooker,"
he said. Do I? NO!

"We must talk about
cheese!" with Ron
Regan, 1982.

Look at the body language! Clearly, I felt closer to Larry, 1981.

Matching haircuts! 1986.

Mr. and Mrs. J.R. Ewing, 1984.

Welcome to the family Ryder! I'm a 52-year-old grandmother! 1992.

Hello, my sweetheart. Dugie, 2015.

Jack couldn't pronounce Grandma so he started calling me Manya. It stuck . . . and that's my name!

The Three Musketeers in London.

Jack, me, Kehly, Jeff, Lance, and Ryder on Mother's Day, 2015.

CUT YOURSELF
SOME SLACK

Once Ed and I sorted some things out with our lawyers, I returned to the house and Ed moved out. Like a lot of divorced men, Ed became an even better father once he was on his own. He really stepped up when the kids were at his condo in Palm Springs on the weekends. They played golf and tore around in the carts. They went swimming and took hikes. The kids loved it.

I made a concerted effort at home to keep things as normal as possible. After filming for ten hours, I rushed home to get dinner on the table, keeping up with my Crock-Pot casseroles for continuity. I kept at them to do their homework and chores. Just as I always had. Meanwhile outside the home it seemed like the whole world was focused on what I wore, whom I dated, and what I ate for breakfast. Fame changed the family dynamic as much as the divorce. I told the kids, "It doesn't mean anything. I'm just a working mom with a camera on me." I tried to keep it as real as I could. If Kehly and Jeff appreciated the normalcy I tried to maintain, they didn't say so. And why would they? Their lives had been turned upside down, and I was undeniably to blame.

Kehly was sixteen when the shit hit the fan. She rebelled in every predictable way, and then some. She blamed me for destroying our family. I was supposed to be a housewife in a housedress, not a TV star.

Our fights were ridiculous and circular, along the lines of:

ME: "Put away the dishes."

HER: "You can't tell me what to do."

ME: "You're living in this house and you have to do your part."

HER: "And if I don't? You're going to kick me out?"

ME: "Do your chores or lose privileges."

HER: "This is *bullshit*! You don't own me! I'm moving in with Dad!"

There was no winning when you gave a gentle warning and the kid came back at you with a bazooka.

During that year, Kehly was openly hostile to two of my boyfriends, sending them running for the hills. She broke curfew, cut school and blamed me for all of it. Oh, and she changed her own name. "I hate my name!" she said. "So many people are named Kelly. How could you give me such a stupid name?" Yes, she'd been born Kelly and she wanted to change it to Kehly, with an *h*.

We called Ed at his condo to discuss it. He said, "Okay, go ahead and change it. But from now on, you have to call us Mohm and Dahd."

Ed and I laughed hard at that. Kehly (then Kelly) didn't find the joke so funny. She hung up in a huff, as only a teenage girl can. A couple of months later, after doing the paperwork herself, she legally changed her name to Kehly. She was very proud of herself, and I was impressed she had followed through.

The new name didn't change her behavior, though. Before she got her license, she took her girlfriends out for a joyride. She sped around Canyon Country and got pulled over by the police.

"Do you realize how fast you were going?" the policeman asked.

"Yeah, but the gas tank is on empty, and I thought if I go faster, I can get home before I run out."

I got the call and went to the police station. Before long I was a regular there. I'd walk in and they'd say, "You, again?" I gave the officers 8x10 signed glossy photos so they wouldn't lock up my daughter overnight.

I was just so overwhelmed by the show and the divorce and the teenage daughter, I didn't know what to do. Frustration got the better of me. Everything I said or did struck Kehly the wrong way. I was so wrung out by the fighting, I tried to ship her off to a Swiss boarding school for her senior year. I pitched it as a great opportunity for her to expand her horizons and experience a new culture in the land of cheese and chocolate.

She said, "You're just trying to get rid of me! Well, I'm not going."

I took her defiance to mean that underneath the rebellion and obnoxiousness, she was still my little girl and couldn't bear the idea of being away from me. Wrong. It wasn't me she cared about. It was my clothes.

Thanks to *Dallas*, I was fortunate to meet some of the world's most talented fashion designers. Valentino. Lagerfeld. My favorite was Giorgio Armani, a charming, generous, classy man. I met him in Milan for a magazine photo shoot. The article was a *Dallas* vs. *Dynasty* fashion story. On one side was Giorgio and me, aka Team *Dallas*. On the other side, Nolan Miller and Joan Collins, aka Team *Dynasty*. (No contest.) I got to know Giorgio and adored him so much I named my dog after him.

All the designers sent clothes to *Dallas* so we'd wear them on camera. Giorgio also sent clothes to my home. One blouse was particularly exquisite. It was white and puffy and magical, and retailed for $950 (around $2,300 today). I wore it everywhere: to parties, out to dinner, on the show. It was a prized possession.

So one day, Kehly came home from school and announced, "Guess what, Mom! I was elected best dressed girl!"

She showed me the picture in the yearbook under the Best Dressed heading, and there was my daughter, wearing my precious Armani blouse. The truth came out. I'd leave the house at 5 a.m. to go to work. Kehly would get up at 7 a.m., raid my closet, wear one-of-a-kind couture outfits to school, and get it all back on the hangers before I came home that night.

It dawned on me that as much as she resented my showbiz life, she craved a spotlight of her own. When I clued into her real feelings, I introduced her to one of the show's producers. Seeing how gorgeous she was, he offered her a small part as Sue Ellen's assistant. Whenever Sue Ellen had a scene at her office—about four or five times that season—Kehly got to stand next to me and hand me papers. The glamorous life wasn't as exciting as she thought. She'd spend hours in the dressing room, waiting to do five minutes of work. Her stint on *Dallas* didn't last long. I was glad to see her go and missed her, the Mommy paradox.

Throughout these rough years in our relationship, I often thought about something my Grandma Betty once told me. We were walking on the beach at Santa Monica and she picked up some sand. She held it loosely in a cupped palm. "Hold your relationships gently, like this. Because if you hold them too tight"—then she closed her fist and the sand sifted out—"you lose them." I guess she would know. She'd been married three times and she buried all three.

When Kehly gave me a hard time for asking her the big three questions (Where are you going? Who are you with? What are you doing?), I once said, in exasperation, "Come back when you're twenty-one and I'll take you to lunch."

If Kehly's life was a soap opera, my son Jeff's was a DIY show on the home channel. Jeff kept himself busy for hours taking apart the washing machine piece by piece and building a darkroom for photographs in the garage. His methodical attention to detail occupied his mind so completely he didn't seem to notice the two women in the house always arguing. He was probably repressing his emotions in an un-healthy way, but I thanked God for it.

Sometimes, though, his reticence was more painful to bear than Kehly's drama—especially the time I missed his high school graduation.

That's not an easy sentence to write, even now over thirty years later.

Timing was to blame. Most of the nine months of shooting per year, we were in Los Angeles. But for one or two months we shot in Dallas, usually in the summer. That June, I was in Texas as expected, but I planned ahead to get home for his graduation, a Saturday. I made it abundantly clear to producer Len Katzman that I needed to be home in time for my son's graduation and was assured I would be.

That Friday we were filming a big scene with the whole cast in it. It just went on and on, and I was staring at my watch the entire time, wondering when I'd get to leave. By 9 p.m., we were still shooting. I'd already missed my flight. The producer announced that we'd have to come back to finish at 6 a.m. the next day.

"I have my son's graduation," I reminded him.

"No. You have to be here," he said. He wasn't forcing me to stay out of spite or cruelty. He just needed to get the scene, and I happened to be in it. He certainly could have shot around me, but he refused. I wished I'd have said, "Screw this," and just gotten on a plane. But I let myself be bullied into staying.

I tried everything I could to get myself back to Los Angeles, even called some of my wealthy Texan friends to set up a private plane. The time difference and shooting schedule just made it impossible. As each possible solution fell apart, my stomach sank a little bit farther. Out of ideas, I called Jeff.

"I'm so sorry, but I can't get back in time for your graduation. I tried everything I could, but it didn't work out. I'm so so sorry, honey."

"Oh," he said.

"If there was any possible way I could be there, I would be," I said.

"Yeah."

"As soon as I can get back to L.A., we'll celebrate, okay?"

"Sure." Jeff wasn't a great communicator and he responded to my apology with monosyllables, which only dug the knife in deeper. I was crushed beyond words. In my place, my sister Betty went to the cere-mony. Ed went, of course. Jeff was glad for the show of family support. But in the end, I was his mother, and I wasn't there. I think he still resents me for it.

Guilt is unavoidable for mothers. It's particularly excruciating for those of us who work. I remember talking to Joan Van Ark about it. We were in the van going to Southfork (before her spin-off *Knots Landing*). I tearfully confided to her that, while I was in Texas filming, Kehly went through an adolescent milestone, something personal and emotional. I cried, "I should have been there."

Joan said, "Do you know how many men are on business trips and miss so many things in their sons' and daughters' lives? Do they cry about it?" Of course, she was right. How many fathers in those days even knew when their daughters got their periods or had their first kiss? How many fathers skipped their kids' graduations for work and made it up to them later with a gift or a special day together? At my high school graduation, my father came and shot a whole roll of film of some other girl he thought was me. He still got full points for showing up. All was forgiven for fathers, but no one cuts the mother any slack. If Dad makes pancakes on Sunday, he's Father of the Year. Meanwhile, Mom packs the lunches and cooks dinner every night and gets no applause for it. Moms, then and now, are held to a higher standard for parenting, even if they're the main breadwinner.

I talked about leaving the show with Joan and other friends. The advice I got most often was something like this: "Why give up your career? You've already done the hard part. They're teenagers and all teenagers resent their mothers. You think they want you, but they want space. They'd rather hang out with their friends than you." My mother wasn't there when I got my period for the first time. She was probably glad I was at my grandmother's. I knew I was a better mother than Marge, but that was little consolation. I still felt like I was letting my kids down.

After that horrible phone call with Jeff, I hung up and asked myself, *How did everything get so messed up?* When I was in Texas or working late in L.A., I was crippled by guilt. When I was home during my hiatus, Kehly and I clashed. Jeff ignored me. Motherhood wasn't fun. Lately, my job wasn't fun, either. I couldn't help flashing back to the night I told Ed I wanted to take acting classes and he said I should wait until the kids left for college. Now Jeff was going off to college. I'd been working for his entire middle and high school years. My life had been dictated by my job. The yoke of it grew heavier every season. Repairing my relationships with my kids seemed a lot more important than Sue Ellen having another fight with J.R., or another affair.

I stuck as close to home as I could that summer and fall. It was clear that both Jeff and Kehly were angry with me, but by and large, I realized that the kids were all right. I hadn't failed them or scarred them for life. They were emotionally sound and more independent than I had realized. I created a false image of myself as a neglectful parent—the Bad Mother guilt was all in my head. My children were no better or worse than the sons and daughters of stay-at-home moms, or working moms with reliable schedules, or married moms, or other divorced moms.

I always hear people say that mothers guilt-trip their children ("You never call; you never write," etc.), but it has been my experience that moms are far more likely to guilt-trip themselves. We obsess about all the mistakes we made over the years as parents and blame ourselves if anything in our kids' lives go wrong.

We don't stop at parenting guilt. Women find fault in ourselves as wives, friends, workers, contributors to society, caretakers of our health and home. We guilt ourselves sick over a million and one things and hold ourselves to impossibly high standards in every aspect of our lives. If we don't live up to the idealized version, we get pangs. If only we tried harder, made more sacrifices, were smarter, more disciplined, slept less. If only we were perfect. I thought I'd shirked my responsibilities as a mom by working. But now I know that I hadn't been fair to myself.

Many philosophers and shrinks regard guilt as a wasted or useless emotion. I think of it as a blinking indicator light signaling that something in your life needs to be examined. If you can take a closer look at the source of your guilt and rationally conclude that you've done the best you could in the given circumstances, then guilt is useless. If you see areas where you can make realistic improvements, then by all means, make them, and eliminate guilt that way.

I wouldn't dare suggest that guilt is easily gotten rid of. It's a habit formed over a lifetime of self-criticism and perfectionism. I was not a perfect mother, wife, or actor. Looking back, I see how hard I strived to be all things to all people and how foolish it was to beat myself up for a few missteps along the way. All of life's unhappiness can be found in the gap between who we think we should be and who we actually are. Perfectionism creates the gap. Guilt widens it.

A good Catholic girl, I can still recite the Lord's Prayer, which I had to do every day at Notre Dame Academy. Regarding the thorny subject of guilt, I often reflect on this particular passage: "Forgive us our trespasses, as we forgive those who trespass against us." If we can expect God to forgive us for transgressions and mistakes, and we're required to forgive the same in others, then surely we can find it in our hearts to forgive ourselves

Henry James once wrote, "Three things in human life are important: the first is to be kind; the second is to be kind; and the third is to be kind." Shedding guilt and accepting our wonderful imperfection is how we can be kind to ourselves, both in hindsight and in the here and now. Forgiveness and kindness are the central tenets to how I live my life. When you look back on events and moments that give you pangs, swap them out for memories and reminders of the everyday accomplishments we never give ourselves credit for.

If you've raced home after working ten-hour days to get dinner on the table every night for twenty years—especially if you brought home the bacon *and* fried it up in a pan—you deserve more than absolution from guilt and the kindness you'd give freely to anyone else. You deserve a gold medal.

HOW TO BE KIND TO YOURSELF

As women, we do so much, and are usually the last on the list of small kindnesses that make a big impact. Here are some little ways to keep our own happiness at the forefront of our minds:

MAKE A VISION BOARD. Years ago, a lovely women whom I admire greatly, Jennifer Butler, introduced me to the color palette that brought out the best in my skin and hair and allowed the focus to be on me and not the clothes I wore. One evening, Jennifer hosted a gathering and invited her friends to create a vision board. We all sat on the floor surrounded by travel, fashion, and design magazines. We cut out pictures and glued them to a piece of poster board that we would later frame. We also added words that fit with our desires and dreams. The vision board is still hanging in my home years later to remind me of the things that are important to me. Of course, they keep changing, just as we do. But it's a lovely reminder to say focused on our desires, whatever they might be. I don't take the vision board with me when I travel. What I do is make a bookmark on plain white strong cardboard, and place the sayings that mean something to me on it using colored markers to make it pop. You may want to do it on both sides, as I do, because I love making it colorful and crowded and yummy. I make several, actually, one for each book I'm reading. Without a vision, people perish. We can't allow our visions to fade or sour. Keep updating and reinforcing them.

BUY YOURSELF FLOWERS. Yep, you are worth it. It doesn't have to be a massive bouquet, just one that makes you smile. Today I went out to my garden and picked a beautiful bouquet of daffodils. I smile whenever I see their faces. Into the house they came and were plopped into a vase. Done. Happiness in an instant. When I travel, I find a local market to buy a bouquet to brighten up my hotel room, too.

GET A NEW LOUNGE OUTFIT. Take a look at your bathrobe or your favorite "go to" outfit you put on when you get home. Do you love it? Is the fabric scratchy? Does it enhance who you are or is it just there? Remember that you are unique and special. You deserve to look and feel your best, yes, even when you're just home alone watching TV. Your mood will change, as will your attitude about yourself. You'll be just as comfortable in something new, and you'll feel and look amazing, too.

TAKE A LONG BATH. I know it doesn't seem feasible when we are rushing to get everything done. But try to carve out some "me time." Turn off the lights, light a candle, and put a few drops of scented oil into the water. The bathroom doesn't have to be fancy. Trust me, I've been on location in some not-fancy bathrooms. When I turn off the light, light that candle, and drop in my lavender, and voilà! The room transforms into a paradise. Put on some relaxing music and let the mind drift wherever you want to go.

TAKE A WALK. When you are taking a stroll, look up. On my daily walks, I notice that everyone else is looking down at their devices. Look up! There's a whole world out there that supports us.

GET A FULL-LENGTH MIRROR. So many women I know leave the house without looking into a mirror first. How you present yourself to the world shows who you are. This is you. Take a good look. Go ahead. I'll wait . . . Now, are you happy with how you present yourself?

GET RID OF CLUTTER. I always say that my eyes need a vacation from looking at "stuff." Piles of paper, magazines, makeup, laundry, books. You probably have your own list. Clear it away and see how you feel after giving your eyes a rest.

DETOURS HAPPEN

Sometime in the late '80s, Larry, his wife, Maj, and I were on our way to Australia to promote *Dallas* and we stopped in Bora Bora for a few days. We stayed in little huts built on stilts over the ocean. You could wake up, walk outside your room, and dive right into the ocean to swim with manta rays and sea turtles. It was absolute paradise. If I had a boyfriend, it would have been the most romantic weekend of my life. But as usual, I was the third wheel with Larry and Maj.

We had a driver, a very pretty young man who I'll call Keanu. So Keanu came down the plank to my hut to pick me up. He was bashful and embarrassed; I wondered if silky-haired Keanu was smitten with me. We collected Larry and Maj, and went to a reception that the mayor of Bora Bora was hosting for us.

Larry noticed that Keanu was missing a finger. "Hey, Keanu. What happened to your hand?" he asked.

"On the island, if you sleep with somebody else's wife, they cut off one of your fingers," he said, and then made eye contact with me in the rear view window.

I tried to imagine being passionate enough about someone to risk a finger to have an affair, and how stupid you'd be to get caught. Not a turn on. Oh, well. No tropical fling with Keanu for me.

We were dressed to the nines. The requested dress code was island chic, preferably bright or white. I wore a gauzy white halter dress. If I so much as looked at a spec of dust, it'd show. Maj wore a flowing white dress and Larry was in a blindingly bright white linen suit.

The party itself was fine. A cocktail and hors d'oeuvre kind of thing. The three of us stood in the center of the room, meeting and greeting, carefully sipping fruity rum drinks.

Keanu waited by the car for two hours until we left. With only hors d'oeuvres in our bellies, we asked him for a recommendation to a restaurant or a beach shack, anything so we could get a bite to eat.

He said, "I know just the place."

We got about three miles when a tire blew, and the car careened off the dirt road and into the ditch. It was dark, no streetlights. The car—a little, junky two-door that had to be fifteen years old—was tilted at an angle with only three wheels touching the ground.

"Everyone okay?" asked Keanu.

We were fine, just a little shaken up.

Keanu tried to drive us out of the gulley. The car lurched forward, but unless we could get that last tire on the ground, we were stuck. He said, "No problem! I'll take care of it." His plan was to go back to the party and get help. He ran back the way we came, and was swallowed up by the dark in seconds, leaving us on the side of the road.

We had no idea where we were and it was pitch black out. It could be hours before Keanu came back, if he could even find us. We laughed about it, but before long, we started to feel nervous. At twenty, getting stranded all night in a ditch would be a wacky adventure. In your forties and fifties as we were, twenty minutes of wacky was enough.

Maj made an executive decision. She got behind the wheel and said, "Okay, I'll steer. You guys get out and push."

"What good will that do? We still have a flat tire."

"We can drive for three miles on a flat back to the party," she said. "Or you can change the tire, Larry. You know how to do that, right?" If Larry didn't, Maj would.

Larry and I got out of the car, went behind it, and started pushing. Maj hit the gas. Some mud splattered up, but the car wouldn't budge. We tried it a few times, but the car just dug in deeper.

"I've got an idea!" said Larry, who was pretty wasted. "Look up that hill. You see that light? Someone's up there. Let's climb the hill, find that hut or whatever it is, and ask for help."

Maj took one look at the terrain, and said, "Great idea. You two go. I'll stay here and wait for Keanu."

She turned on the headlights so we could see a little bit up the hill. Larry and I head toward the light. I was in heels, in the dark, crawling up a mountain. Somehow we managed to get to the hut, which was actually a tree house. We had to scale wooden planks nailed into the trunk as a kind of ladder. We made it up to the thin landing and knocked on the door.

A woman opened it, took one look at us, and started screaming bloody murder. She was howling at the top of her lungs, mouth wide open.

She started pointing into her house, still screaming. We were able to lean into the door and see what she was pointing at. The TV was on and Larry's face filled the screen. She was watching *Dallas*, and then suddenly, J.R. and Sue Ellen appeared at her door, in a tree house in Bora Bora, late at night.

"I can't believe this!" she screamed.

"Tell me about it, darling," said Larry.

By now, the woman's poor husband, who'd been sleeping, was wide awake and trying to figure out what was going on.

"Who are you and why are you covered in chicken shit?" he asked.

I looked at Larry. He was smeared head to toe in what, as it turned out, was *not* mud. His white linen suit was now brown. Larry started to laugh. "Linda, darling, you've got something on your dress."

As it turned out, we'd gone off the road outside a chicken farm. Like a gravitational force, I was constantly being pulled, against my will, into yard bird poop. I couldn't escape it. In a previous life, I must have been a coyote.

We explained the situation to the man, who, it turned out, was the electrical engineer at our hotel (no wonder they had power in their tree house). I asked, "I know it's late, but would you drive us back to the hotel?"

He said, "I don't know who you are and you smell like crap."

Larry and I begged. His wife begged, too. The guy relented. We all climbed down the ladder and went to his pickup truck parked nearby. "You have to get in back," he said, holding his nose.

As directed, we climbed into the truck bed. We drove back to the road and found the car. Maj was invited to sit up front with our savior. Keanu was still nowhere to be found.

When we got back the hotel, I said, "Thank you so much for helping us. Can we buy you a drink?"

We arranged to meet back at the hotel bar in half an hour, giving him time to go home and get his wife, and for us to shower and change. An hour later, we were eating and drinking in the bar, having a great time. Larry was in fine form, charming the engineer's wife and turning the gathering into a party, as he always did.

Well into the fun, Keanu wandered into the room, looking like he'd been to the wars. He got lost looking for the original party, but managed to find someone to help him dig out his car. He sat down next to me at our table, took my hand in his, and said, "Ms. Gray, I was terrified I'd never see you again. I realized tonight that I'm in love with you and want to marry you. Give up your career and come live with me on my thirty-two-foot sailboat. We can travel the world!"

Hmm! I was tempted, I have to say. I wondered if he'd feel the same way if he'd seen me an hour ago caked in crap.

Larry and Maj stared at us like their teenage daughter had just been propositioned. The engineer shook his head. His wife beamed at me, hoping I'd say yes.

"Keanu, you're very sweet, but we've only known each other for two days," I said.

"When you know, you know." That attitude was why he had only nine fingers.

I didn't marry Keanu. But I'll never forget him, or any of the details of that hilarious night. It's one of my favorite memories of Larry and Maj, and perfectly illustrates why I loved them both so dearly. When I look back at my life, I treasure the times I veered recklessly off track, when well-laid plans were dashed. I cherish the happy disasters, when things seemed to go horribly wrong, but somehow, wound up being so wonderfully right. Every snafu is a story in the making. Getting lost is how we find our sense of humor and sense of adventure. I'll take getting covered in shit with beloved friends over a staid cocktail party any night of the week, regardless of what I'm wearing.

STEER THE BUS

In 1985, after eight years on *Dallas*, my contract was up for renewal. I came to the negotiation with a very short list of demands. I didn't care about money or how many lines I had. What I really wanted was to *direct*.

I was the cliché of the actor who longed to get behind the camera. Larry and Patrick had been given the privilege, and it seemed like they were having a lot of fun in the captain's chair. I knew it wouldn't be an automatic "yes" for me, a woman, so I was sure to get some experience under my belt before I even brought it up with the powers that be.

The year prior, I studied technique with Lilyan Chauvin, a French actor and director. Directing isn't just making a square with your fingers and saying, "Action!" You have to block each scene, know where to put the camera, when to get your ECU ("extreme close-up"), when to get a wide shot, how to interpret the script, how to move the camera to heighten the tension. For example, in Alfred Hitchcock's *Marnie*, he first focused in on Tippi Hedren's canary yellow purse and then broadened the shot to show the rest of her. Why? The audience immediately had to know, *What the hell is in that purse?* That's suspense.

Lilyan taught me the skills. The human element would be more instinctual. Some directors had a gift for getting great performances out of the actors. I knew I'd excel in that department. Having worked alongside the cast for years, I knew their strengths and weaknesses. I was a pretty good listener and spoke respectfully and sincerely (thank you, Dale Carnegie).

So I walked into the room to negotiate my new contract with Leonard Katzman, recently promoted to executive producer. I said, "Here's the deal, Len. I don't want any more money. I'll sign up for season nine and ten at the same salary I have now if you let me direct just one episode in fifty-six shows. I've been studying with Lilyan Chauvin. You let Larry and Patrick direct. Now it's my turn."

"No," he said. "That's not going to happen."

"I'm prepared to leave the show."

"Okay."

"Okay, I get to direct?"

"Okay, you're fired."

I left the room in tears. I was furious.

I called Lilyan, who started cursing in rapid-fire French, lots of *"merde!" "connard!"* and *"salaud!"* I was using all the English equivalents and then some. It was a total slap in the face. Len was willing to cut me loose because I'd asked to do something that had been handed to male actors without question or hesitation.

I called Larry. "I just got fired," I said. "It's been a great eight years."

Larry went ape shit and stormed into Leonard's office. He said, "If Linda goes, I go!" Larry loved playing the knight in shining armor. I appreciated the gesture (no way in hell would he *really* have left the show), but I wished he didn't have to ride to my rescue. Why should either one of us have to threaten to quit? It was so infuriating.

Lawyers got involved. The calls went back and forth between my team and the producers of the show. I just wanted to know why. Why was I denied the opportunity that he'd readily bestowed on Larry and Patrick? The answer was, "If Linda directs, then all the women will want to."

It was like saying, "If one woman works outside the home . . . if one woman speaks her mind. . . if one woman runs for office . . ." The idea of a woman in power jarred Len's sense of right and wrong. I'd gotten along with him okay until then, but during those negotiations, everything changed.

Leonard eventually caved, sort of. His capitulation wasn't much of a victory for me. I signed on to do seasons nine, ten, and eleven at my old salary, and to direct one out of eighty-four episodes.

It sounds crazy. Why would I agree to that? I might not have been acting with a cool head. At first, I wanted to direct for the creative outlet, to expand my repertoire and to make Lilyan proud. Also, I was kind of bored with Sue Ellen after eight seasons. All she did was drink and have affairs. At first, Sue Ellen's struggle was culturally relevant. But women were changing. The world was changing. The audience and I both wanted more for her. If I had power and influence behind the camera, I could push for changes in front of it as well.

When Len shot me down, all my creative intentions went out the window. The primal scream started blaring in my head. I would've agreed to anything to direct. I couldn't walk away. My personal pride wouldn't allow it. I'd studied; I'd come prepared. And I was not going to let a chauvinist keep me from proving it.

Directing turned out to be just as wonderful as I had hoped. When I showed up for my first day of filming the episode, I found a big, white, old-fashioned megaphone in my director's chair. Larry had gotten it, and had everyone on the cast and crew sign it for me. It was lovely. Everyone was rooting for me, and I didn't let them down. After that battle, I was not going to fall on my face.

It was a challenge to direct myself acting. I'd set up the shot, and then run to do my lines. I had to climb up a ladder in my high heels and big shoulder pads to line up the shot, and then scramble back down to act in the scene. Everyone looked toward me to make the decisions. I'd never been given that much authority before. I liked it.

My first episode, called "Just Desserts" (so perfectly titled) aired March 14, 1986. Ten days later, a landmark article in the *Wall Street Journal* coined and explained the term "glass ceiling." I took pride in the fact that I'd shattered mine.

Not only that, my show got great ratings. It was an excellent episode, if I do say so myself, and millions of viewers tuned in. Why? I sold the hell out of it. I went on every talk show that would have me and touted my directorial debut. I was not shy about taking credit and telling fans that it wasn't easy to get the job, that I made it happen, and it's fabulous.

Even Len had to admit that my episode was a hit and masterfully directed. He came to my trailer and said, "Well done, Linda." It wasn't an apology for trying to block me. It wasn't an admission that he was wrong. It certainly wasn't an offer to tear up that contract and give me more money. But I know how to accept a compliment when it comes my way.

I said, "Thank you, Len. Now that all the ugliness is behind us, I want to direct. Again."

I wound up directing four episodes, all ratings hits. Since Len wasn't able to say, "Thank you" at the time and since he is now deceased, I'll say, "You're welcome" in absentia.

When my contract came up for renewal again, I didn't sign it. Directing helped me get through my final years, but only just. The truth was, I was winding down on *Dallas* for years. The show started out as my salvation. It was a gift from the universe that I accepted with my whole heart. But a decade was long enough to do one job, to portray one person. It wasn't an angry or bitter decision, and there was no rancor on either side. It was just time for me to go.

My final scene was shot in Culver City on the soundstage. It was in the living room of the Ewing residence and I wore a beautiful Thierry Mugler royal blue suit. I said my last line. The director said,

"Cut." The camera crew moved into the dining room set for the next set scene and I stood there, frozen on my mark.

I'd lived this character for eleven years. I'd loved and adored her, and nurtured her like a child. And I'd never see her again. It was like my life flashed in front of me and I remembered everything that had transpired since 1978. I played through all of it, every change I'd been through personally and professionally, in an instant, and was overwhelmed. It took me awhile to compose myself and go back to my dressing room.

There was a swell party later that night, and I celebrated and grieved Sue Ellen's life and times. I mark that moment alone in the Ewing living room as the end of an era. I was forty-nine years old and ready to make some changes in my life, and, if possible, in the lives of other women as well.

For the last thirty years, columnists and writers have tracked the thinning of the glass ceiling. In Hollywood, it is still very much in place, especially concerning female directors.

There are so many cracks, though. When I was asked to join the cast of *Dallas* 2.0 in 2011, I was excited to see the name Cynthia Cidre on the script. Cynthia developed the reboot, produced it, and wrote it. A woman was in charge and I breathed a sigh of relief. I knew my character and the show would be in good hands with a talented woman at the helm.

Feminist consciousness is still rising. If you just look around, you'll notice that women are at the forefront and stepping up in every area of life. We are leading with our hearts. We are remembering our own innate intuition, our imagination, knowing that being in control and having power is our birthright as much as it is for any man.

Almost every woman I talk to lately says the same thing to me in a different way: They welcome challenges and responsibilities. But they're exhausted and they don't have time to do all the things they are supposed to do, have to do, want to do. Their days are packed and they need to go on a long vacation. Women are living on vapors masquerading as energy.

Recently, Oprah Winfrey, a very busy woman, told Jimmy Fallon, "My life was going from the next thing to the next thing. After a while, it feels like a blur. That's why, particularly now, I try to take a deep breath and take things in." When Oprah says she needs to slow down and savor the moment, we should listen. Enjoy the harvest of our good work. We've achieved so much. We need and deserve to pause and take it all in.

I'm as guilty as anyone for taking on too much. I promise myself each year that I'll get more vacation time. And yet, I usually say "yes" to new opportunities. While writing this, I was in a play, and all my lines were rhyming couplets. I had to memorize page after page of poetry. It was weeks before I felt comfortable with the material. But I did it. I forced myself to learn something new, and I could feel my brain synapses lighting up. Working keeps me sharp. Ideally, we can alternate periods of hard work with recuperative reflection. I don't think Oprah pauses for too long before she moves on to the next thing. As I grow wiser, I slow down enough to enjoy my life, but I don't ever stop.

TREAT EVERY RIDE LIKE IT'S THE LAST ONE OF YOUR LIFE

The night before I directed my first episode of *Dallas*, I was up late, strung out, and stressed. I nearly quit my job over this opportunity and I was not going to screw it up. I sat cross-legged on my bed, papers fanned out before me, a dozen lists on yellow legal paper, the script covered in annotations. I'd checked and rechecked every item on my lists. I'd made a million notes. I was ready for anything.

The phone rang. It was Betty. We talked a few times a week.

"Calling to wish me luck?" I asked casually.

"Of course! Break a leg on your big day tomorrow," she said.

I heard something under the words. "What's going on?"

Betty took a rattling breath, like she'd been crying. "Linda, I have breast cancer," she said and then broke down.

It was six years since a drugged driver killed my niece, Leslie. It hadn't been an easy time for Betty or her husband. Losing her firstborn and only daughter sent Betty into a downward spiral. If it weren't for her son, Mike, maybe she would have drowned in sorrow.

Now tragedy had come again. She told me that she went to a doctor because she'd been feeling sick to her stomach a lot. During the exam, her doctor discovered a mass in her left breast. He sent her to an oncologist who was brusque as he examined her and started pressuring her to get a mastectomy and begin aggressive chemo immediately. "He yelled at me," said Betty, who was terrified enough and didn't need a "healer" to bully her.

"He sounds like a prick," I said. "Don't do anything until we find someone you're comfortable with."

I was in shock. My baby sister had cancer. She was only thirty-nine. Shock helped me, though. If terror and grief set in right away, I wouldn't have been able to get down to business. I shoved the papers off the bed. What had been an obsession two minutes ago now felt completely inconsequential. I got out a fresh legal pad and started making a new To Do list. Item number one: Call Nancy Brinker.

Through friends in Dallas, I'd met Nancy Brinker, an incredible woman who, in 1982, created a foundation to find a cure for breast cancer after her only sister died of the disease at thirty-six. Her sister's name? Susan G. Komen. In years to come, Nancy's little foundation would raise nearly two billion dollars. She'd survive her own bout with the disease and in 2009, be awarded the Presidential Medal of Honor by Barack Obama. Back in 1985, when Betty was diagnosed, the foundation was just starting out, but if anyone could help Betty find a supportive oncologist it'd be Nancy.

Betty ended up talking to and liking Nancy's own doctor, who happened to be in Dallas. By the date of her surgery, I was already back in Los Angeles. I went to Texas for her operation, but I couldn't stay in Dallas for her first round of chemo. I was glad she loved her doctor, but being so far from her home base made it harder for Betty. Our parents were back in Palm Springs, and her husband and son were in Los Angeles. I'm sure we could have found a doctor closer to her support system, but Betty did what she wanted to do. When I couldn't be with her, we were in constant touch. I sent her weekly care packages with cute sweat outfits, food she could hold down, and wigs, but it was still challenging for her not to have all of us around her.

My brother-in-law, Tim, reacted to Betty's cancer by deciding to train for a marathon. He literally ran away from reality. It's an understatement to say that I was angry with him. But he didn't know what to do or how to help. Men need to be educated on how to deal with the practical and emotional demands of having a wife with cancer. When a woman loses her breasts, she fears that she's lost her femininity. A reassuring husband would have been a tremendous help to Betty and the entire family.

She went into remission briefly. After two rounds of chemo, she had a couple of months of relative good health. I remember her calling me on her fortieth birthday to say she went on a great bike ride. Just feeling well enough to go outside in the fresh air was a triumph. It was her last great ride. When the cancer came back, she tried half a dozen treatments, cycling between hope and dejection, in and out of hospitals until she died three years later at forty-three.

By the time you get to be my age, your life will be touched by cancer. Either you'll have it or someone close to you will. There will probably be a death, if not several. Cancer has cut through my life like a scythe. The diagnosis day was only the first step down a dark, steep stair. Each step gets colder, bleaker, and scarier. In the end, Betty talked about seeing Leslie again, and that was a comfort. Betty worshipped her daughter, and the feeling was mutual. When Betty lost her, a shadow sank into her skin. She did her best to compensate for her grief, but it was always there. A tragedy that profound imprints on your being. Six years later, it seemed like Betty's grief turned into a disease. As terrified as she was to die, I suspect that Betty longed for the pain of Leslie's death to end.

Seeing someone so vital, so young, slowly slip away is wrenching and goes against the natural order of things. It just seems wrong. I've tried to see how Leslie and Betty's deaths fit into the big picture. Of course, young people all over the globe die horribly, through no fault of their own. But when someone close to you dies tragically, it still seems unfair. We're often told, "life is unfair." Death is unfair, too. I spent this past Christmas at the home of a friend in London and had dinner with her ninety-year-old mother. This woman was sharp as a tack, no glasses, no dentures. Why did she get to live so long in such good health when my niece was struck down at seventeen and my vibrant sister taken at forty-three? Luck of the draw? God's will? I don't have a clue why some get to stay and some don't. Ideally, our friends would stick around and we'd get to play with them until we all passed peacefully in our sleep at one hundred. We can't understand our mortality. We can only love as hard as we can while we can for the limited time we have, and grieve our losses.

For me, the grief continues. Betty was my best friend. She was the only person on Earth to truly understand me. We grew up in the same house, in the same bedroom, and shared values, secrets, and parents. Unlike a lot of sisters, Betty and I weren't rivals or jealous of each other. We were partners, cohorts, two halves of a whole. At times during childhood, our home life was tumultuous. We were each other's rock, the safe place to stand as a river raged around us. There's no one in my life I can speak a thousand words to with a glance. Nowadays, when I talk to women about their sisters, I have to swallow the lump in my throat. It's been over twenty-five years since Betty died, and I still reach to call her first when I have news. I'll never get over the loss, but I've figured out a way to benefit from it. I've found the silver lining in the darkest cloud.

When things go wrong, I remind myself that Leslie never got to worry about her career. She never got to try bangs, or go abroad, or debate the merits of organic cooking. Betty didn't live long enough to go gray, or worry about her viability in the workplace, or get wrinkles.

Every day you're alive is a gift. It might not seem that way when you're in the throes of the flu or an emotional tangle with your daughter-in-law. But it is. Just this week, I came home after two months in London to find that due to a power outage, my refrigerator switched off, turning the food in my freezer into sludge. So much food wasted. I may have to replace the unit to the tune of $3,000. But I'm grateful for the luxury of being alive to deal with it. It's taken me decades to appreciate sorrow, annoyance, and disappointment as life affirming. Instead of sweating the small stuff—and the big stuff—I shrug and say, "thank you."

THE TRAMPOLINE
EFFECT

For a couple of years after I left the first run of *Dallas*, I remodeled my home and drove myself a little nuts with too much time on my hands. I did some TV movies—what, you don't remember *Highway Heartbreaker* and *Moment of Truth: Broken Pledges?*—but I always had my eye out for a new regular gig.

One day, I took Kehly to a doctor's appointment and while I sat in the waiting room, I noticed a tiny paragraph in *Variety* about Aaron Spelling's new show in development, tentatively titled *Models Inc.* The plot would revolve around Hillary Michaels, the ruthless boss/mother hen of an agency. Spelling was considering Joan Collins, Linda Evans, Farrah Fawcett, and several others for the lead.

Where's my name? I was not on the list. Wasn't I on par with the other sirens from the big hair, big shoulder pads '80s era of TV drama? My feistiness kicked in and I called my agent, a bit in a snit.

"Can you get me an appointment for Aaron Spelling's new show?" I asked.

"I can't," she said.

"If you don't, I will."

"He wants a movie star."

"Well, I want this job." The character was a single mother, no husband, a strong woman, on her own, running a modeling agency. The character and I inhabited the same universe. I knew all about being on my own, having a difficult relationship with my daughter, plus I'd logged a lifetime in the modeling world. I convinced my agent to make the call anyway and snagged a meeting.

At the Spelling Empire mothership, I was shown into a conference room, thinking I'd meet Aaron and a few chief lieutenants. The room was filled, standing room only, with at least thirty people. It was intimidating. I was apparently interviewing with Spelling's entire staff.

I sat down and Aaron started talking about the character and the show. I explained all of the things I had in common with Ms. Michaels, and rehashed a few of my adventures in modeling back in the day. I reminded the full house that I'd been on *Dallas* for eleven years, and still had a passionate fan base. Then I said, "I have a sense that you want a movie star. The problem is that the pace of movie acting isn't the same as television. They can spend an entire day shooting a two-minute scene. I've been trained in TV. I know the timing and pacing. I memorize fast and can deliver on a dime."

I knew that was going to appeal to Aaron's interests. Time was money, and to make an hour-long drama every week, you had to be fast. The meeting ended after about thirty minutes. I got in the elevator. When the doors opened in the lobby, my phone rang. It was my agent, telling me that I got the job.

Another series! I was thrilled. Spelling was riding sky-high at the newish Fox Network with one hit after another, including *Beverly Hills, 90210* and the red-hot *Melrose Place*. In fact, the first step for me as Hillary Michaels was to do a four-episode guest-starring arc on *Melrose Place* as Heather Locklear's mother.

When I made my *Melrose* debut, Kehly and I watched it together on the couch in the living room, a bowl of popcorn between us. When I appeared on screen, we cheered. I thought I looked good and delivered my juicy lines well.

Kehly quieted me so she could hear the dialogue. As an obsessed fan of the show, she didn't want to miss anything. I watched her watch me, and felt a surge of love and appreciation for my daughter. When the show broke for commercial, she said, "Now you've arrived."

Forget my eleven years on *Dallas*. It wasn't until I strutted into her favorite show that Kehly respected me as an actor. It was surprisingly gratifying to earn her approval. I hadn't realized how badly I had longed for that. Every night for the next couple of weeks until my *Melrose* arc ended, we watched the show on the couch or on the phone together.

One might describe *Models Inc.* as the most hotly anticipated show of the summer of 1994. It was hyped by the Fox and Spelling machines for months. Audiences and critics expected another delicious and debauched drama with the nutty Spelling recipe of glamour, madness, mayhem, and sex.

They were all sorely disappointed. We flopped. Right out of the gate. Some of the coverage felt like a mean-spirited attack. We did a preview event for network affiliates that was covered by press, a mini-fashion show of the cast in Escada, strutting down a runway. Debra Gendel, a fashion reporter for the *Los Angeles Times*, wrote, "When actress Linda Gray took her bow at the end of the show . . . one woman snipped: 'She looks like she's tired of smiling.'" She went on to theorize that I was miserable to be among all the young lovelies (including a pre-*Matrix* Carrie Anne Moss), and that in comparison, my hair and wardrobe were dowdy.

Critics were savage about the actual show, and my performance in it. Ken Tucker's review in *Entertainment Weekly* was especially hard to read. "[*Models Inc.*]'s major casting problem, I'm afraid, is Gray. [She's] doing something odd with her mouth these days; she seems to be trying for some cross between an insincere smile and a predatory grin, but it always looks as if someone has wedged an invisible harmonica between her lips." The worst part: He wrote that he wished that Farrah Fawcett had been cast in the role instead of me.

Critics renamed it "Models Stink," and threw shade on every aspect of it. The writing. The actors. The depiction of the modeling world. No one was spared. You could always say, "At the end of the day, it's all about the writing." But I believe it's our job as actors to turn whatever's on the page into magic. Then again, there are limits to what you can do.

When a show is a hit, it's the result of a thousand pieces fitting together seamlessly, plus great writing, plus pure luck. It has to capture the zeitgeist of the moment in just the right way to earn fans and respect for critics. When a show's a flop, it can mean just one element was out of place. *Models Inc.* was a fantastic fiasco, and I bore the brunt of it. It wasn't the first show to get a lot of hype and then flame out in spectacular fashion (as it were). It would certainly not be the last. But for me, having come from *Dallas*, and having campaigned hard for this job, it was a pretty far fall from grace.

Mainly, I was embarrassed. *Dallas* had been universally loved. *Models Inc.* was universally mocked. Even though we knew we were toast, we had to keep reporting in for work, week in, week out, and attempt to breathe life into a walking corpse. Logically, I knew that failure pushed you off the wrong path and toward the path you're meant to be on. Clearly, I was not meant to be on *Models Inc.* The show was cancelled after one season.

I think of bouncing back from defeat as the Trampoline Effect. You go low, and then, inevitably, you bounce back up. The Trampoline Effect worked in slow motion for me that year. I'd been so elated to land the job and to impress my daughter. The media build up was long and sustained, and I was bouncing up and up for months. When I came down again, I had to wallow while I worked, finishing out the required number of episodes before we put the show out of its misery. It wasn't fun, that's for sure. But I focused on giving it the best I could, and not embarrassing myself further by phoning in a performance. I'd heard once that you were judged not on how you behaved when you started a new job, but how you acted when you were on the way out. I swung for the fences to preserve my dignity and professionalism. That was my solace.

When it was all over and I had time to reflect and slowly rebound to a normal state of mind, I reflected on what had happened, going back to the beginning.

We all fail at some point. But we can choose to fail with grace. The circumstances are irrelevant. You can fail spectacularly in public, in front of God, the *Los Angeles Times*, and everyone you know, or you can you fail in the privacy of your own mind. To be a successful failure, all you have to do is marinate on the key questions:

What did I learn from this experience?

What can I take with me into the future?

What were the positive aspects of it?

If we don't learn the lessons, we're doomed to repeat our mistakes. They'll come back stronger the next time, and keep coming until we deal with them.

What I concluded about the *Models Inc.* disaster: My campaign to get that job wasn't about loving the script, which I hadn't seen. I wanted to work with Spelling, who was a hit maker. I hoped to make a big, splashy comeback. From the first moment I read about the show in *Variety*, I was motivated by ego.

Talk about the humility of self-awareness.

I don't view failure as a negative. It's neutral, just a thing that sometimes happens. Of course it might sting for a little while, but then you get over it. After you've logged your share of failure, you stop thinking that every one will be your last. Not true! Most of us have an unlimited potential to fail, just as we have an unlimited potential to succeed. Without our failures, we wouldn't learn from our mistakes and the successes wouldn't be possible.

Post–*Models Inc.* and the ego revelation, I concentrated on the work that really mattered to me, that struck a chord in my mind, soul and heart—not my ego. If I haven't matched the success (in superficial terms) of *Dallas*, I have matched the joy and pride of genuine, organic creativity many times over. On the road to happiness, authenticity is the only measure of success.

CHERISH YOUR
PASSENGERS

Ever had an experience that was truly shocking? One that made you question reality as you know it? I have.

It started when, around New Year's in 1991, my daughter Kehly, then twenty three, invited me to tea at the Hotel Bel-Air.

That alone was a shock.

Just a few years before, she'd have sooner invited me to my own beheading than an afternoon tea. The truth is, since her weddings to Lance, our arguing had dropped off precipitously. Yes, weddings. Not a typo. She had two.

The first was in Puttaparthi, India, at the ashram of the guru Sai Baba. The groom's father was a devotee of the healer, and Sai Baba himself was going to officiate the wedding. To get there, the entire wedding party would have to take three flights and ride for hours across the subcontinent in a rickety bus. I thought, *Nothing is easy with this kid.*

When we arrived in Puttaparthi, I learned that our nuclear family—Kehly, Jeff, Ed, and I—were assigned to one room. We'd have to sleep on cots and share a bathroom. Ed and I weren't the best of friends, so it was immediately tense. On the plus side, the ashram was beautiful. Everyone wore colorful saris and the women had elaborate henna tattoos on their hands and feet. Kehly and I got them on our toes. I couldn't have them on my hands because I had to bathe her (see below) and I had to be Sue Ellen Ewing again in a few days. (I was directing an episode.)

The night before the wedding, the guru's acolytes came to our room and said that it was traditional for the mother of the bride to bathe her daughter before the ceremony. It was a symbolic act, that I'd give my child one last bath before I handed her over to her husband. So at 5 a.m., Kehly and I got up, went into our little bathroom, and I splashed water on her, really doused her. We were giggling and flinging water at each other.

Sai Baba's sister helped us get dressed. I wore a traditional red and white sari; Kehly's was a Technicolor dream of oranges, pinks, and reds with strands of gold. The sister had a long braid down to her waist. She cut it off and pinned it to Kehly's hair, symbolizing something very important. It was so touching, but also bizarre that Kehly would be wearing a stranger's real hair at her wedding ceremony.

When I left after the beautiful ceremony, I was jealous that Ed got to stay in India with the newlyweds to travel around the country with them. I had to go back to work to direct the Ewings, my TV family. On the plane home, I worried about Kehly. I liked her husband, but she seemed too young to get married (although she was around the same age I had been when I got married). I remember thinking, *Will I ever stop worrying about this kid?*

Her second wedding was in Los Angeles on Halloween for the friends who couldn't make it to India. It was at the same hotel where we would meet for tea the next year. We decorated with white pump-kins, and white swans swam in the water under the bridge the guests crossed to get to the ceremony. Kehly's gown was magnificent and she was stunning in it. The bridal party wore black velvet dresses. Mr. Hagman came in a Merlin outfit, because of course he had to outshine the bride. Kehly had taken to married life like a swan to water, and my relief was palpable. I'd been holding my breath for the last year, hoping that, despite her young age, her union with Lance was real and lasting.

So when she invited me to tea that day, my first thought was, "She's going to drop a bomb on me."

We sat down and Kehly handed me an envelope. I opened it to find a birthday card. "It's not my birthday," I said, thinking, *My own daughter doesn't know my birthday?*

"Open it," said Kehly.

I did. She'd written a note that read, "My due date is September twelfth."

My birthday.

"Your due date is my birthday?" I said, still not getting it. A split second later, the cylinders in my brain fell into place. My baby was having a baby.

My eyes filled with tears. I was so overwhelmed with joy I couldn't speak. I jumped out of my chair and hugged her.

I was sobbing, and trying to talk, and finally managed to ask, "On my birthday, really?"

"Almost like we planned it."

It was shocking that Kehly was so calm, but she amazed us all throughout her pregnancy with quiet confidence. She took the body changes, morning sickness, and mood swings in stride. If she wanted to, she could be a professional pregnant person. My wild child had morphed into a responsible adult. I couldn't have been more proud of her.

On September 10, Kehly called and said, "I'm in labor. Get over here!" After nine months of placidity, my daughter was starting to get nervous.

Hearing the panic in her voice, I started to feel some of my own. I

got in my car with my "grandma bag" and sped over to her place, driving 80 mph, freaking myself out by driving so fast. I concentrated on
the road ahead. Out of the corner of my eyes, I saw something in the
windshield in front of the passenger seat, like a reflection.

It was a boy. He was wearing a little striped t-shirt and shorts, with
blond hair and brown eyes. He started singing, "*Happy birthday to you,
happy birthday to you . . .*"

With my heart in my throat, I managed to get control of the car,
thinking of the headline the whole time: "*Dallas* Star Linda Gray Dies
in Highway Accident While Speeding to Her Pregnant Daughter."
Driving at 50 mph in the slow lane, I looked again at the image in the
windshield.

The boy was still there.

"Can you sing again?" I asked.

He disappeared.

I told myself I'd had a stroke or gone temporarily insane, which,
oddly, was a relief. When I got to the hospital with Kehly, I might
have someone check my eyes or listen to my . . .

"*Happy birthday to you . . .*"

He was back, and now he was laughing. This time, I pulled over.
But when I put the car into park, he was gone.

It was a California code of conduct to explore the woowoo side
of life. I'd been to psychics, tarot card readers, astrologers, past life
regression. I'd had my human design and horoscope mapped, explored
energy work, various meditation techniques, and been acupunctured,
Reiki'ed, and shiatsu'ed. Few people could be more wide open to the
mystery as I was. But I had never experienced anything as vivid, intense, and jarring as this. A full-blown, well defined vision with sound.
He appeared clearly as day and sang "Happy Birthday" to me twice,
moving his little hands like windshield wipers.

Now you think I'm completely crazy.

For the rest of the ride, I was afraid he'd come back even though I wanted him to. My hands were shaking on the steering wheel. When I got to my daughter's, I must have looked a bit crazed.

She was ready to go right to the hospital right away. I suggested that, instead, we take a walk. Along with my vision, I received an understanding. My daughter was not going into labor today. My grandson had appeared to me and he told me that we would meet two days hence, on *our* birthday.

"You're acting weird," said Kehly.

"I'm excited to be a grandmother."

I didn't dare tell her the truth or she'd want to put me in the hospital. But she agreed to take a short walk. We made it around the block once and her contractions stopped. "False alarm," she said, but I knew that already.

I stayed over because Kehly was convinced the baby would come that night. During the night, we did make a hospital run when she felt a contraction. The doctor examined her and sent us home. The next day, while taking another walk, Kehly complained about the waiting. I said, "He'll come when he's ready."

"You think it's a boy?" She and her husband had decided to wait to find out the sex.

"I *know* he's a boy," I said. "He has blond hair and brown eyes."

"Mom, you sound like a witch."

Maybe I was. I'd had a psychic vision. As every long hour ticked by, I could feel him growing brighter and bigger, his soul shining and ready to burst into the world.

Ryder arrived on September 12, in the wee hours. The first sounds he ever heard were his whole family singing, "Happy Birthday" to him in the delivery room, along with sobs of joy and laughter.

In the coming weeks, whenever Ryder got fussy, I'd sing our song to him. His eyes grew big, and recognition kicked in. It was as if he thought, *Hey, I know that tune*, and he'd quiet down to listen to it. Holding my grandson, the greatest gift anyone could ever receive, I felt the psychic connection flow back and forth between us, and I imagined he felt it, too.

The biggest shock of all: Kehly turned out to be an amazing mother.

A few months after the birth, Kehly and I took Ryder to the mall at Sherman Oaks. I pushed his stroller. Kehly walked beside me, occasionally reaching into the stroller to fuss over the baby. She was a doting, loving mom, so together, so responsible. I was awed. Only ten years ago, we were fighting tooth and nail. Now we were strolling together with this beautiful baby. I was so struck by it, I stopped and said, "I want you to know, I never thought I would see this day."

"What day?"

"This. Just pushing around your baby at the mall."

"You didn't think I'd become a mom?"

When I played through "Kehly's future" scenarios in my head, "suburban mother" never came up. I just hoped she wouldn't wind up in prison. I smiled at this ratty teenager all grown-up and looked into the same eyes that used to shoot daggers at me. "Tell me about Ryder's poop today," I said. Only a grandmother cared as much about a baby's poop as his mommy. We kept our conversation in the present and didn't go back to our contentious past. We were together in the joy and peace of the moment.

Kehly is forty-eight now and she tells *me* what to do. "Update your blog!" and "Tweet a link to your new show!" She's a working mother like I was (am), with two kids—Ryder, now twenty-three, and Jack, eleven (our baby, my heart)—and an executive job with the Los Angeles Kings. She and Lance are still happily married.

I don't worry about her anymore.

Ryder is all grown-up. He's a bona fide adult, with an apartment and a career in photography. Our connection is still strong, as is our tradition of spending our day together every year. How many twenty-three-year-old men want to hang out on their birthdays with their grannie? Not many! Ryder is the gift that keeps on giving.

Last year, we had breakfast together and then went to the Museum of Contemporary Art, Los Angeles. Kehly joined us for lunch there (interloper). After she left, Ryder and I went shopping on La Brea, one of his favorite places, and he let me spoil him with presents. For dinner, we drove to Venice, ending up at Intelligentsia Coffee at 10:30 p.m., where we talked for hours about life. It was a fantastic, perfect, glorious day.

Parenting wasn't what I expected. It was just what was expected of me, a woman of my time. I was supposed to get married and push out some pups. I struggled with the confines of motherhood when my kids were young—loving them through my personal dissatisfaction. Later, I fought to define myself apart from motherhood, not because I loved my children less, but because I had to love myself, too. My life changed, and I loved them through their anger and through some of my own. The parent–child dynamic was so complicated, with a lot of ups and downs. It's never easy and not always fun.

Grandparenting, on the other hand, is a simple, pure, uncomplicated marvelous delight. The love springs fully formed from your heart the moment you hear the news that your baby is going to have a baby of her own.

I had a vision of my grandson, but I couldn't have envisioned the joy Ryder and Jack bring me. Being a grandmother has redefined my capacity for love, and it continues to expand the boundaries every day. It makes me a little dizzy to imagine the seismic force of the love I'll feel when I have great-grandchildren.

(Hint, hint, Ryder. But no pressure!)

LINDA GRAY'S
PRINCIPLES
FOR SUCCESS

Hello, Reader! You sure look lovely today, Reader! I hope you're enjoying my book. It goes down really well with a glass of red wine and a Crock-Pot casserole. But you've probably figured that out already, in your infinite creativity and intelligence, Reader!

Dale Carnegie would approve of how well I've mastered his 30 Principles for Success over the years. I feel capable of talking to anyone and have even expanded on his list to include some principles of my own, based on awkward, heart-breaking, and emotional conversations I've had over the years with hard-to-please people in challenging situations. Such as . . .

#1: When in Doubt, Ask About Kids and Pets

A few years ago in Dallas, I was filming a pivotal scene when John Ross, Sue Ellen's only child, committed her to a sanitarium (like father, like son). The shoot was supposed to be eight hours, but went for fourteen. I'd been invited to attend the "Dallas Does Chanel" fashion show at Neiman Marcus that night, and the party afterward. Karl Lagerfeld would be there, along with fashionable VIPs from Paris, New York, and Los Angeles. As per my "play more!" code, I wanted to go to that party!

When the shoot was *finally* over at 9:30 p.m., I couldn't go directly from the set to the event, though. My wardrobe in the scene was a pair of gray sweats, with no "Sue Ellen" hair or makeup. I'd been crying on demand for hours and my eyes and hair were a puffy mess—nowhere near the level of style I'd need to hang out with Lagerfeld.

I'd already missed the fashion show completely. If I rushed, I could make it to the end of the party. Two of the show's hair and makeup artists, Charles Yusko and Frieda Valenzuela, worked on my head for three minutes. Afterward, I drove like a bat out of hell to my condo to get my dress. Meanwhile, my publicist, Jeffrey, made arrangements to send a car to pick up me up there with a coat and an evening bag (Chanel, of course).

I arrived at the party at 10:30 p.m., way beyond fashionably late. As my car pulled up, a string of limos were pulling out. I ran into the room, and realized that all the muckety-mucks, including Anna Wintour from *Vogue*, were long gone. The room was nearly empty. Karl Lagerfeld's publicist introduced me to a few people who'd stuck around. I was going on fumes by then.

We came up on a tight cluster of male models in the back of the room. Karl himself was at the center of it. I was amazed and delighted he was still there. As I approached him, the photographers who'd already started packing up their wares whipped their cameras out and pointed them at us.

Karl put out his gloved hand and said, "*Bonsoir.*" We kissed on both cheeks, but it seemed rote. Was he annoyed I was so late? Maybe he was as exhausted as I was. The camera trained on us, I hoped the pictures wouldn't show two tired, strung out people, not the picture of fun and happiness.

I had to lighten and brighten the mood, so I asked, "*Ou est Choupette?*" His cat.

Karl smiled and said, "À *l'hôtel avec Nanny.*"

We both took out our phones and showed each other kitty pix and chatted in French about Dugie's elegance and Choupette's fluffy adorableness. What could have been a tense talk turned into sweet *tête-à-tête.* We kiss-kissed again, and he left. The photo that ran in the papers was of us smiling and looking like the best of friends. Which brings me to my first Principle: When in Doubt, Ask About Kids and Pets.

#2: Take a Deep Breath, Focus and Listen

Enid Borden (former head of Meals on Wheels and current president and CEO of the National Foundation to End Senior Hunger) and I went down to Richmond, Virginia, together to chop celery and carrots to prepare daily meals for needy seniors in the area. Enid was an inspiration and so passionate about her cause: feeding the "hidden hungry" in America, the poor elderly. She was making a documentary about it, and I was only too happy to help.

After packing the meals, we loaded the van and set off to deliver them with the film crew. The first woman I met was around eighty-five, and all dressed up for her moment in the spotlight. I sat on her couch and she showed me photos of her family, most of them far away or deceased. Next, we visited a man, a veteran, who'd dyed his hair black for our little video. We sat on his stoop for a spell and he told us stories about World War II. Florence was one of our last stops. She was ninety, housebound, and impoverished. She had *nothing.* The documentary people had to buy her a dress to appear on camera. We sat on her back porch and talked about her life. I was overcome with sadness that this delightful, sweet woman, if not for Meals on Wheels, would go all day without eating. She received one meal from us a day, her lunch. No one would be bringing her breakfast or dinner.

I was a senior, feeding seniors, in America, land of plenty. Florence lived in Richmond, not Rwanda. Most of us don't realize that there are hundreds of thousands of elderly people right at home who lack the ability or resources to feed themselves. I didn't, until I worked with Enid. Just sitting with them, handing them food, and listening to their stories was a life-changing experience. It was hard. But I learned to Take a Deep Breath, Focus, and Listen. Then Go Back to Your Hotel Room and Cry (aka Principle #3).

My friend Linda Evans heard about what we were doing for seniors, and we joined forces. She flew to Washington, D.C., and we appeared before Congress to discuss the issue. While testifying, we were sure to Pull No Punches (Principle #4), and followed Principle #5 (Don't Sugarcoat Needlessly). Unless you stand up and shout about your cause, no one will bother to listen. We urged our representatives to remember the seniors, not to push them off a cliff. Most people don't give a crap about old people, other than their own family members. But if the family is gone, what can they do? Starve to death? The measure of any society is how well we care for its most vulnerable citizens. If you can't pack and deliver meals, buy a homeless person some food. Volunteer at a shelter. Write a check. Do anything to improve the lives of those in your corner of the world. It starts with awareness and it ends with compassion.

Principle #6: Check Your Face Before You Sit Down to Eat With People

I have a koi pond in front of my house. It's got a dozen real beauties that have been my pleasure to feed for twenty years. An interior designer named Waldo Fernandez gave me the idea. He also came up with a brilliant notion of knocking out a wall when I was redesigning my kitchen. The new space was beautiful and we were both very proud of it.

So one day in the early '90s, Waldo called and said, "Can I bring a friend over to your place for lunch to show her the kitchen?"

I was a bit taken aback, but I said, "Okay. Who's the friend?"

"Elizabeth Taylor."

O-kay. It's not every day a living legend comes to your house for a meal. "Great. When?"

"Forty-five minutes."

Naturally, I had nothing in the house and no time to go shopping, so I scrambled in my pantry to figure out what to serve Elizabeth Taylor for lunch.

I ran out to the garden and picked some spinach, sautéed it with garlic and tossed it in some pasta with sauce. I got the food ready with enough time to slap on some moisturizer and blush.

So they arrived and I served Waldo, his partner Trip, Ms. Taylor, and her assistant Liz, some pasta. She sat across from me and was just as glamorous and stunning as you'd hope. I was dazzled and tried not to stare.

While talking and eating, Trip started to kick my foot under the table, and brush at his face when I looked at him, as you do when you're trying to tell someone they've got food on their chin. I dabbed my napkin, but Trip kept doing it. I thought, *What the hell? I can't be eating that sloppily.*

We finished the meal and Waldo gave Ms. Taylor a quick tour. After they left, I went to the bathroom. I looked in the mirror. My entire face was peeling. I looked at the counter and realized I'd put on a facial mask instead of the moisturizer. From that day forward, I always think, "Check Your Face Before You Sit Down to Eat With People (#6)."

What could I do but laugh? I'd been sitting across from the most beautiful woman in the world and my face was peeling. Trip called the next day and said, "Thanks for lunch. But what was going on with your face?"

I must not have made too freakish an impression. A year later, Trip and Waldo took a summerhouse in the Hamptons, and invited me for a weekend with Calvin Klein, some Hollywood people . . . and Elizabeth Taylor. She walked into the kitchen with a white dog and said, "It's the bitch with the long legs!"

A term of endearment. I was grateful she didn't say, "It's the bitch with the flaking face!"

She was fabulous, a bawdy broad with a dirty mouth and the face of an angel. She liked me, which was unusual. Apparently, she didn't tolerate women well, preferring to hold court with men—gay, straight, both, didn't matter as long as they had balls. The reason she was okay with me? I had balls, too, and Refuse to Take Shit From Anyone (Principle #7). One day, we were in the kitchen, and she said, "Linda, get me some orange juice."

I said, "Get your own orange juice."

She started laughing that great laugh of hers, just like in the movies.

Principle #9: Drink the Wine (Even If It Looks Like Piss)

Dan Gordon, a famous screenwriter (*The Hurricane* and *Wyatt Earp*) and playwright (*Irena's Vow* and *Rainman*), came to me with an idea for a movie. He wanted to update *Now, Voyager*, with me in the Bette Davis role, and Ms. Davis as the mother. I was very humbled at his invitation and said, "I'd love to, but how will you get Bette Davis?" She was my hero, my acting role model, an extraordinary woman. I didn't think she'd consider taking the supporting part in a remake of her classic film. Dan put out feelers and, incredibly, she was interested.

That week, I had an appointment with José Eber. I told him about the movie. Of course, he knew Ms. Davis (he did her hair) and offered to make introductions. He took a photo of me and sent it to her. This was her thing. She liked to see pictures of people before she considered meeting them.

A few more days went by. I was in the kitchen feeding the cat, and the phone rang. I answered it, spooning out tuna, and I heard, "Hello, Ms. Gray? This is Ms. Davis. Let's make a film."

I nearly threw the cat food across the room. My idol was on the phone! Talking with the *voice*! And she wanted to work with me.

I was too stunned to speak, but I got out, "Okay."

"My assistant, Kathryn, will set up a meeting." Then she hung up.

I was invited to have cocktails with her. José informed me that the cocktail was a test. If I didn't bore her, she'd invite me to dinner.

José and I drove to her summer home in Malibu. I brought her a box of gardenias (camellias were out of season). We were shown into her opulent living room by Kathryn. After a few minutes, a tiny, frail woman walked in. She'd just gotten out of the hospital a few days earlier.

"Hello. Nice to meet you," she said, clipped, with that *voice*. I got to listen to it for a half an hour over wine and champagne as we chatted as a group. Then Ms. Davis took me toward a private window seat, sat down with me, and said, "Let me tell you what I think of every cast member on *Dallas*."

As it turned out, she was a fan, which mortified me. She'd been watching me *act*? I could never compare to her. I tried to stay calm as she went though the entire cast and told me who she thought they were in real life. She was spot on; it was scary. Then she said, "And you, my dear, are too nice. You let them push you around. On Monday morning, this is what I want you to do. I want you to walk on to the set and I don't want you to speak to *anybody*. You go in, and sit in the makeup chair, and don't talk."

I said, "But we've been doing the series a long time. I know everybody and we are all friends."

"*Don't speak to them*," she said. "At first. Then gradually bring them in. If you start off friendly, it doesn't work. If you bring them in gradually, they will be yours forever." I wasn't sure I agreed, but it was a Principle worth considering, and borrowing.

She went on to explain that she never let anyone in. She watched, listened, and observed, and then, if they dared, they could come in *slowly*. Not everybody. She was very discerning. "I don't like everybody, and I don't have to," she said.

Apparently, I made the dinner cut. Ms. Davis directed us into José's car and we drove to a restaurant in Malibu. Making an entrance with Bette Davis might've been the coolest moment of my life. We sat down and she ordered white wine. To the waiter, she said (in the voice), "White wine looks like *piss*. I don't want it. I want bourbon. But my doctor took me off that, so I have to drink the stuff that looks like piss."

The waiter was a bit shocked, but he brought the bottle. Since Ms. Davis didn't like to drink alone, we were encouraged to Drink the Wine (Principle #9), too. I would have quaffed actual piss to keep her talking. Throughout the meal, she took cigarettes out of the silver holder that Kathryn held open for her. It was so dramatic to watch her smoke those unfiltered cigarettes. She told story after story, cigarette after cigarette, for hours and hours. She had just gotten out of the hospital and told us all fabulous stories of being there, holding court no doubt, and of all her amazing actor visitors. It was heaven.

The movie never happened. I didn't care. I was just so grateful for that one night with her.

Principle #10: Listen With Your Whole Heart

In Nicaragua, as a United Nations Goodwill Ambassador, I went to a birthing clinic. On every bench and bed, a young woman was in labor. Most were teenagers and didn't seem happy about having a child. The post-natal moms sat in beds with blank stares and babes in their arms, wondering how they would feed and nurture them. Some shared their fears with me, that if they complained to their husbands about not having enough food or proper shelter, they'd be beaten or abandoned. Among the hundreds of moms, I saw only one or two dads.

I was talking to one girl with a newborn son and a very handsome young man kept peeking around the corner at us. I asked if he was the father and she nodded. He agreed to join us, and I asked him what he wanted to do with his life. He said, "Go to college in the United States." I turned to the Mom and asked her the same question. She just cried. Her mother had already gone to America to work as a housekeeper to send money home to her family. Now the father of her child was planning on leaving, too. She said, "I'd like to go to college, too," but we all knew that wasn't going to happen.

There was nothing I could say to her to fix an impossible situation. All I could do was Listen With Your Whole Heart (#10), Don't Judge (#11), and Empathize (#12). You can't help everyone, but if you open your heart, they'll feel your compassion. Their gratitude will flow right back into you. Caring and listening won't change someone's practical problems. But it can relieve them of a bit of the burden, even if only temporarily. We do what we can.

Principle #15: Say "Cheese!"

I was invited to a Presidential State Dinner in 1983, but I hesitated about attending. Just divorced, I didn't want to go alone. Kehly said, "You were invited to the White House to eat with the President and King Fahd of Saudi Arabia. You're going!"

We went to Neiman Marcus and Kehly talked me into buying a Valentino strapless black dress and a beaded jacket to go with it. It was the most expensive outfit I'd ever purchased, at $2,200.

I stayed at the Four Seasons in Washington, D.C. A hairdresser did my hair for the dinner. He asked to see what I was wearing. I showed him my dress and said that I intended to take off the jacket after dinner. He said, "No! You'll be in the room with King Fahd and you can't show skin." Oh, well. The jacket would stay on.

Protocol insisted I have an escort, so they sent a marine in full uniform to the hotel to pick me up. He brought me into the White House ballroom. Sigourney Weaver, Peter Martins, and Pearl Bailey were there, too, along with a thousand other people, all elegantly dressed. You could feel the power in the room. Suddenly, a man came up behind me, took hold of my arm, and said, "You're going to be my dinner partner."

It was George H.W. Bush, vice president. I said, "With pleasure."

What does one talk about at dinner with the vice president? I thought I'd have to discuss high-level politics, but we chatted about the usual: kids and pets (aka Principle #1). At one point, the VP looked across the room at a sexy woman in a cleavage-baring dress (clearly, that woman didn't get the King Fahd no-visible-skin memo). He said, "I am with the classiest woman in the room."

I said, "Thank you," to Graciously Accept A Compliment (#13), even if it was kind of awkward. Which reminded me of another Principle: Don't Trash Another Woman's Outfit at a Party; It's Just Rude, and Doesn't Make Your Dress Look Any Better (#14).

Later that night, I met President Reagan and the First Lady. I thought, *What do you talk about with the leader of the free world?* I didn't break out the usual ("How're Lucky and Rex?"), and instead, went a bit off point and brought up surplus cheese. I don't remember anything about our conversation because I was so hot in my beaded jacket, and completely overwhelmed. But a few days later, I got a letter from the president. "Dear Ms. Gray: Thank you for expressing support for the release of surplus cheese to the needy," and promised he'd get right on it.

I do recall that after the First Couple left the room, I was disappointed I didn't get to take my picture with them. And then, five minutes later, they came back, walked right over to me, and posed for the photographer. Then they left again. The photo had a political purpose: Texans were Reagan's base. No way was he going to miss an opportunity to pose with a star of *Dallas*. I smiled, as one does.

I left alone, minus my Marine, and reported back to Kehly that it was a fabulous night. She said, "You're welcome."

LINDA GRAY'S PRINCIPLES FOR SUCCESS

1. When in Doubt, Ask About Kids and Pets
2. Take a Deep Breath, Focus, and Listen
3. Keep Your Emotions in Check Until You Can Go Back to Your Hotel Room and Cry
4. Pull No Punches
5. Don't Sugarcoat Needlessly
6. Check Your Face Before You Sit Down to Eat With People
7. Refuse to Take Shit From Anyone; They'll Respect You For It
8. If You Start Off Too Friendly, It Doesn't Work. If You Bring People in Gradually, They Will Be Yours Forever
9. Drink the Wine (Even If It Looks Like Piss)
10. Listen With Your Whole Heart
11. Don't Judge
12. Empathize
13. Graciously Accept a Compliment
14: Don't Trash Another Woman's Outfit at a Party; It's Just Rude, and Doesn't Make Your Dress Look Any Better
15. Say "Cheese!"

THE DANGERS OF DOWNSHIFTING

One of the big myths about aging is that you have to slow down. The metaphor is that you speed through youth in high gear and then continually downshift in old age, until you're basically crawling with cars blasting their horns behind you.

That has not been my attitude. I've kept working long past the official retirement age of sixty-five and have tried my hand at nearly every aspect of acting. I've been part of a touring company in Europe, driving around in a bus from hamlet to village square, and performing *The Graduate* in the West End. I've been in a slew of TV movies, made guest-starring cameos in TV series, and done short films and feature films. I've done live theater. I even did a stint as a soap opera actress, with a recurring role on *The Bold and the Beautiful*. (Now that was an education in down-and-dirty acting; I had to memorize twenty pages of dialogue every day for ten episodes. Major props go out to soap actors. They're the quickest studies and hardest workers in the biz.)

I see acting as an endless education. I've been fortunate to meet different talented, devoted people along the way, and to learn from every experience, bask in the gratitude, and appreciate them all. I have no intention of slowing down, professionally or intellectually.

I know many people in their sixties and seventies who have down-shifted. First, they retired from their jobs. Then they moved to Florida. Then they stopped exercising, and traveling, and entertaining until all they do is sit around their condo watching TV and complaining about the neighbors. One woman I know does nothing for herself. She has a housekeeper to clean, orders takeout for every meal, has some-one come in to organize her closet. She shops online instead of going to stores and when she does venture out, she always drives. She lives in a senior community down South, and takes the car three blocks from her condo to the pool. Her attitude is, "I've got the money to have other people do my chores for me. I don't have to walk if I don't want to. So why should I?" She's seventy-five and creaks around like she's ninety. Every day she melts deeper into the couch, waiting for and being waited on by other people.

She's downshifted her life to a dead stop.

Look, I'm not a big fan of scrubbing floors, either. But if you refuse to do the simple things for yourself, you become what you most fear about getting older—dependent, weak, and inefficient.

If you make your own dinner and clean your own bathroom, you'll get to cook meals and squeegee your shower walls for many healthy, happy decades to come. Even chores become empowerment exercises, little ways to strengthen muscles and sharpen the mind. Washing and chopping vegetables seems like a pain in the ass every night. But over a lifetime, you'll develop excellent knife skills. If you buy pre-chopped, you gain nothing.

Downshifting grinds away your passion and energy. Never stop try-ing new things and doing small mundane tasks—and appreciating your ability to do them. Otherwise, life really does become a waiting game, but you're not waiting for a train or an appointment. You're waiting for nothing, the void. To combat that, just say, "What am I waiting for?" get up and do something, anything that gets you moving and in the world.

You don't have to know where you're going. In fact, it's better if you don't. We all know what it's like to travel in a foreign city and get lost on your way to the restaurant recommended in the guide-book. You stumble upon a hidden gem that turns out to be more fun and memorable than the place you intended to go. Or you go into a store to buy a dress and wind up finding a cozy sweater you treasure for decades. I've learned to be open to the unexpected. Serendipity is everyday magic. You can help it along with a sense of adventure. You never know what hidden gems and lucky finds you'll stumble across.

The tiny bistro might have the best food you've ever tasted.

The organic grocery shop woman named Gerry might be your fairy godmother.

Stay open. Don't get locked into anything. When you venture out into the world, turn left instead of right. Get lost and you might come home with a miracle.

HOW TO GET MOVING

Like my beauty tips and breakfast menu, I've often been asked about my fitness routine. I do the occasional class and some stretching. But mostly, I walk. Every day, I walk outside for forty-five minutes. Here's why:

FOR MY BONES. Being outside gives me all the Vitamin D I need, which helps my body absorb calcium. Unlike many women, I don't take drugs. I prefer to treat myself naturally with sunlight, and a course of vitamin and mineral supplements recommended by my doctor after he's done my annual blood test and urinalysis. If I'm deficient in any-thing, my doctor tells me how much of each supplement to take, and which foods to eat to boost my levels. It's vital for women not to just self-medicate and gobble pills randomly. A blood test costs around

$50, and depending on what you have tested, will give you a wealth of information about your health.

FOR CIRCULATION. You might've heard "sitting is the new smoking?" Whenever you sit for long periods of time, you cut off circulation to your backside and your lower limbs, which can cause clots, fluid build up, weak muscles, cellulite, and the list goes on. The rule of thumb (toe?) is to stand up or take a short walk for five minutes for every hour of sitting. I've made a habit of standing whenever sitting isn't required. When I talk on the phone, I get on my feet. I often read with the book on the kitchen counter, so I can do it upright. If I'm waiting at an airport, I walk around instead of just plopping down. Even if you can add fifteen minutes of standing time per day, you'll get your blood moving. Otherwise, I jump on a rebounder and do certain yoga positions like downward facing dog and legs up the wall to get the blood flowing in different directions.

In Los Angeles, we have spas with far-infrared saunas, which don't feel as hot as a regular sauna but increase the toxin output in your sweat by six times. I also use a dry brush—only ten dollars—before I shower to bring impurities to the surface of my skin, and then rinse them away. In the evening, I take an Epsom salt bath (about one cup) with baking soda (about half a cup) thrown in and sip my hot tea with a sprinkle of cayenne. The salt and heat gets my blood moving, as does alternating hot and cold showers. And, get a massage as often as possible—a small luxury. If you can find it, a lymphatic drainage massage helps reduce bloat and really gets your fluids coursing like a mighty river.

FOR JOINTS. Before and after my walk, I do some stretches. You have to open up the hips, and lengthen ligaments and tendons. Along with my daily stretches, I take movement classes with my friends to keep the joints limber. Fish oil supplements are like WD-40 for your joints. I like Krill Oil. I take a few capsules a day to keep them lubed.

FOR MUSCLES. It's a bit hilly where I live, so my forty-five minutes of walking hits all the muscles in my legs, the quads when I go downhill and the hamstrings when I go uphill. I speed up and slow down to hit different parts of my calves and hips, too.

FOR MY HEAD. I call the morning stroll my Gratitude Walk. With every step, I give thanks for the beautiful sky, the mountains, and the clean air that fills my non-asthmatic lungs. I give thanks for my ability to give thanks, for my beating heart, for my family, and my wonderful life. I give thanks to my grandfather, who taught me that you can do anything, no matter the challenge. Leave the phone at home!

GIVE

After my London stint last year, I was exhausted and completely burned out. Two shows a day, every day, for eight weeks? I was seventy-four, and had never worked harder in my life. We were all exhausted, no matter what age we were. I barely made it out with my wand and tiara intact.

When I got home, I decided to go to a spa for a week to refresh and rejuvenate. The middle-range place I usually go to was fully booked. A room was available at another place, much pricier. I got a quote and thought, *Wow. That's a lot.* But I booked it anyway. Not only that, I loaded up my schedule with massages and treatments. If they suggested something, I said, "Sure, why not?" When I got the final bill, my jaw hit the floor. It was a fortune! In one week, I'd made a serious dent on what I earned doing *Cinderella*.

How much? It was expensive—but not as expensive as a funeral.

As desperately as I needed to relax and be pampered after working so hard, I still felt guilty spending the money. But then I gave myself a little lecture: "You brought joy to so many people doing this play, all the little girls who came wearing princess dresses and tiaras. You made them happy, and you deserve to be happy, too. You earned it."

I also reminded myself of the takeaway from a book that I keep on my nightstand to reread, *The Richest Man in Babylon* by George S. Clason. His rule is to give yourself ten percent off the top of any paycheck. If you earn $1,000 bucks, peel off the first $100 and spend it on yourself before the bills, before the kids. I have to remind myself of this rule often. I really do have a hard time spending money on myself. I've lived in the same house for forty years—except for those few months in Malibu. When I did flee then, I was able to do so because I planned for it and had the reserves to make it happen. I don't shop often, and am always conscious of what I can afford. If I don't have the money, I don't go shopping. Looking back, hesitating before purchasing has given me financial freedom now.

Money is freedom. Money is fun. But when you think of money as a measure of your worth, you're on shaky ground. I learned this by reading *The Seven Laws of Money* by Michael Phillips. The takeaway for me in this classic is that money is an illusion. We look at the number at the bottom of a balance sheet to feel secure or happy or accomplished. But as a measure of our self-worth, money is meaningless. Your value as a human being has to be more than the bottom line. Don't use it as a yardstick for yourself, or others. And don't view your fee for a specific job as a measure of your worthiness.

Many of my financial habits and attitudes were picked up and reinforced by reading *Money: Master the Game, Seven Simple Steps to Financial Freedom* by Tony Robbins. Robbins interviewed scores of financial wizards to get their secrets of investing and accumulating wealth. It's a good go-to guide of practical rules for getting, keeping, and growing what you earn. I also have a wonderful financial planner who oversees my IRA account, but I don't intend to retire. The very idea is not in my realm. When I take my least breath, that'll be my retirement.

When I decided to direct a play, *Murder in the First* (written for me to direct by my friend Dan Gordon), at the Rubicon Theatre in Ventura, California, I worried about taking on this very time-consuming job for no money. On the way to the theater that first day, I drove by strawberry fields in Oxnard and saw the people picking the berries, and thought, *They're making more money than I am.* I was directing the play for nothing, a labor of love. I just felt incredibly blessed. I needed that reminder that I was privileged to get to choose to work for free. This job was a great big gift I gave to myself. I needed the experience. And I wanted to push myself creatively. It wasn't about the money. In fact, I knew that nothing that was really important to me had anything to do with money.

I'm well aware of what is commonly known as Bag Lady Anxiety. It's a real, recurring dread for forty-nine percent of American women across income, age, and marital status barriers. The Allianz Insurance Company asked over two thousand woman ages twenty-five to seventy-five if they feared losing all their money and becoming homeless. Among single women, fifty-six percent were afraid of one day living on the street with all their possessions in a shopping cart. It's an irrational fear, but it exists nonetheless, probably because the idea of being hungry, homeless, and alone wraps three primal human fears into one dirty, moth-holed blanket.

The cure to Bag Lady Anxiety is generosity. As my grandmother used to say, "When life gives you lemons, give lemonade to someone who's thirstier than you are." No one ever went broke from sharing his or her wealth. Any act of giving will enrich your life beyond measure. It doesn't take much. I've seen acts of extraordinary generosity among the society women I've met in Texas, geniuses at raising thousands and thousands of dollars for their causes. You don't have to write big checks or go to Africa to distribute medicine to sick children. Any act of generosity, no matter how small, creates a ripple effect that changes your outlook on life and the entire world. Whatever takes you out of your own head and allows you to focus on another person benefits you both.

I aspire to love as deeply as I can, and to give everything I have. Love and Give. In midlife, we tend to be go-getters. In late-life, we can be go-givers.

A great quote from Rumi: "Yesterday, I was clever and I wanted to change the world. Today, I am wise so I'm changing myself." I noticed the big shift in my thinking about giving when I went through the Change, menopause. It didn't alter my body nearly as profoundly as my mind and attitude. It brought out a real need to share. I stopped getting my period and all of a sudden, emotions and experiences flowed out of me. I started speaking openly about my life, things I'd held back forever. That was when I first realized I had wisdom to offer. I had time, energy, money, and love to offer, too. I had to give whatever I had to for my own sake, as well as others.

I noticed that the Bag Lady survey didn't include women over seventy-five. It was probably an oversight, because my generation is usually the first one the media cares about.

That was a joke, by the way. We're the last ones people turn to for insight, which is such a shame. We have the most of everything to give. To me, at this stage of life, all wealth comes from within. I can't buy anything that will make me feel as happy as looking at my grandsons' faces, or taking a walk on a sunny day. Life is abundant, and the wealth of the universe is just waiting to be collected by each one of us. We are all together on this planet, free to bask in the abundance of nature and each other's generosity. My children are your children. Your children are mine. By giving to others, you give to yourself.

WHAT TO TAKE
WITH YOU
WHEN YOU GO

After our divorce was settled, Ed and I went our separate ways and called a truce. The cause of our problems—being married—was eliminated. It took a few years, but eventually, my anger, resentment, and frustration toward him dissipated.

At first, our interactions were awkward. When we had to see each other, I wasn't sure what to say. I had no intention of being the cranky one. If anyone was going to be a bitch, let it be Ed. But he wasn't. He was his usual self, keeping it light, skimming on the surface, not daring to dip below to the emotional depths. And for once, I was grateful for it.

When Kehly was in labor with Ryder, I was in the delivery room. After Ryder was born, Ed came in, and we held our new grandson together. We looked at this beautiful child and at each other, and in one glance reached an understanding: No matter what, this child was going to benefit from our amicable relationship. For the happiness of our entire family, we found peace. I have friends who went the other way, refusing to let go of their anger, their ex rage dominated family gatherings and ruined special events. Weddings had to be organized around warring factions, and timetables created for visiting new babies. Everyone suffered when exes clung to resentment. That would not be us.

The Christmas after our second grandson, Jack, was born, Ed came to my house to celebrate Christmas with Kehly, Lance, and the boys. We served dinner together and worked as a unified team to make the holiday special for everyone. We had a wonderful time. It was proof that attitudes can change. You can choose to forgive, move on, and drop the block of concrete you carry with you whenever you are in the same room as this person.

We weren't BFFs. No double dates or brunches on the weekends. But we were comfortable, at ease, and equally besotted with our grandchildren. We sat next to each other at many recitals and family gatherings. I even looked forward to seeing him at Little League games. Like me, he never remarried.

In 2005, we'd been divorced for twenty years. But I was still among the first to find out about his colon cancer diagnosis. He was given four months to live. He dug into his German stubbornness about following a strict Western protocol. A friend of mine told me about a clinic in Puerto Rico run by the former head of oncology at Johns Hopkins. He wouldn't hear a word about my wackadoo alternative bullshit. (After I cured him of "nervous stomach," you'd think he would have jumped right on it). I got in touch with the doctor anyway and he sent me links to videos about the nutrient infusion regimen and faxed me information about his clinic.

I knew that Ed would reject the treatment as crazy if I pushed it on him. So I just forwarded a few key links, and sent some papers to him. He followed the trail of crumbs I left for him and looked into it.

He had to feel like he'd discovered it himself. It was a little trick I'd learned to play in our twenty years of marriage. It worked. One day, he said to me, "I researched this clinic and I'm going to give it a whirl."

He and his sister flew to Puerto Rico for a week, and he would return twice more during the course of his illness. The doctor prescribed a change in diet (Ed had reverted back to his old ways after our divorce), and a lot of supplements. His four months stretched to six, then a year, then two years. He made excellent use of that time, devoting himself to the kids, his grandsons, and his many friends.

The cancer came roaring back, though. Ed and his sister (who was now living with him as his chief caregiver) moved to a rented cabin by the water of Big Bear Lake. His family used to go there when he was a kid, and he wanted to return to the place that had given him such joy. The kids and I drove two hours most weekends to see him, help with care, and just hang out.

He started fading. A hospice caregiver was asked to come to the lake. His friends knew the end was near, and started arriving at the cabin to say their good-byes. That last weekend felt like a reunion.

Ed announced that he wanted bacon, which was not on his approved food lists. He gave me a look, as if I might deny him pork product in his last days.

I said, "What the hell? Let's make some bacon."

He smiled and said, "What the hell."

So we fried up a mess of greasy, fatty bacon, and he ate as much as he could (not that much, but he loved every bite), and then said he wanted to take a nap. His friends cleared out, and his sister drove into town for supplies. Just the four of us—Ed, Kehly, Jeff, and I—the core, were left in the house. I was on the porch; Jeff was in the kitchen on his computer. Kehly was reading in Ed's room.

I looked out at the water, and it got really quiet.

"Mom," Kehly called for me.

Jeff and I ran in. We stood around the bed, holding hands with Ed and each other. And that was it. Ed left. We cried, blessed him, and sent him on his way. It was as if he'd been waiting to be alone with us, his nuclear unit, together again one last time. Those final seconds were healing for Ed, for all of us. The universe gave us that gift. It was a glowing, quiet, precious moment that I will never forget.

When people come into your life, they leave an imprint. Husbands and lovers may leave our lives; they also leave their imprint behind. That's why they are never far away. If they were there for a day or for decades, they will show little glimpses of themselves throughout their lives and beyond. Being with Ed at the end was a bit like catching many glimpses of him in an instant, all of them beautiful.

Even when death is peaceful, like Ed's, with minimal pain, surrounded by his family, in a beautiful place with a belly full of bacon, it's still hard to say good-bye. It always will be. Grief can be softened by the clarity of death, though. In the middle of life, we often hold tight to anger, resentment, and bitterness. But at the end, they're so obviously pointless.

Five years later, in 2011, I got a call that changed my life. A team of producers was going to reboot *Dallas* for a new generation, and they wanted Patrick Duffy, Larry Hagman, and me to reprise our roles. Of course, most of the new cast would be comprised of young hotties, but we were to be the anchors of the series. The three of us had been best friends for thirty-five years, and we were thrilled to work together again after a twenty-year hiatus. Like kids, we were on the phone with each other, giggling and giddily making plans. Patrick and I knew Larry wasn't well, but playing the character he loved so much would give him a shot in the arm.

The producers, Michael Robin and Cynthia Cidre, invited us to dinner, and they were smart and talented, everything we'd hoped. They wanted to shoot the entire show in Dallas, unlike the previous incarnation that shot mainly on a sound stage in L.A. "So when would you like to start?" one of them asked us.

In unison, we all said, "October!" then started laughing. The three of us had endured enough scorching Texas summers to last a lifetime. I expected the three of us to be on the same page. I was stunned that the producers had asked us when we'd like to shoot. It was unheard of! The talent is never given choices like this. Usually, you get a call sheet with instructions to report to such and such a place at this date and at this time.

Larry hosted a meet and greet for the cast at his condo in Santa Monica before we left L.A., so we could break the ice with the actors who would be playing our sons, spouses, friends, and rivals. Maj was not in attendance. She'd been diagnosed with Alzheimer's and was in an assisted-living facility. Larry had a lot on his plate, but he put on a good face. Larry was a gracious host, but he couldn't remember who anyone was. Every time I circled back to him, he'd ask, "Now, darling, which one is my son again?" I just remember laughing and laughing and feeling so happy for this second chance with Sue Ellen, and to be working with my pals.

So we went to Dallas and got ourselves set up in condos for the six or seven months of shooting. My apartment was charming, a two-bedroom on a high-floor in a luxury tower. I feathered our nest in the sky and Dugie, my cat, and I got quite comfortable there.

When Larry arrived on set, he looked awful. Fifteen years earlier, he'd had a liver transplant, but this was something else. He told Patrick and me that he had throat cancer.

My intuition said, "Call that nutritionist." A friend of mine had recommended a Dallas-based nutritionist named Nancy Addison if I happened to need one.

I called Nancy and told her about Mr. Hagman. "He's got diabetes, a transplanted liver, and cancer, and he's going to start filming a TV show for eight hours a day."

Nancy said, "Is that all?" She was kidding, but didn't sound intimidated by what we were up against.

She and I met to discuss Larry over lunch. She was wonderful, a fount of information, and I hired her on the spot. When I got back to the set, I told him, "I got you a nutritionist. You are paying for it. She's blonde, a Texan, and a great cook."

Larry couldn't resist a blonde Texan. He said, "Bring her over."

Nancy started cooking for him. I was her sous chef. We chopped a lot of veggies on Larry's behalf and forced them down his throat. With supreme nagging, we got him off sugar and alcohol. Whenever he saw me coming, he'd roll his eyes like I was the champagne police. But he stuck with the program. He loved all the attention, and his health was improving.

Maj's situation, however, was getting worse. She kept escaping from the home she was living in, so Larry moved her into an apartment with round-the-clock care. In the middle of the night, she snuck out and started banging on the neighbors' doors. Larry flew home with his assistant to check on her. Although they'd been married for fifty-seven years, Maj had no idea who Larry was. (It's been two years since his death, and she still has no idea. But she's happy. She loves to garden, so her kids and caregivers just keep giving her plants to put in the ground.) It was devastating for Larry whenever he saw her, but with the distance—her in Malibu, him in Dallas—his visits were particularly rough.

On his flight back to Texas, he drank four glasses of cabernet.

Cancer and chemo had weakened his body, but not his rebellious spirit. We'd have to get him back in line. Nancy and I served him his dinner that night as usual. We ate our meal together. When he finished, he asked, "Great. Now what's for dessert?"

"The four glasses of wine you had on the flight," I said. "You're diabetic. That's enough sugar to kill you!" He was furious at his assistant for ratting him out, and annoyed with me for calling him on it. I sat down and said, "You have a second chance here to do the role you were put on this planet to play. Everyone is so happy to see you again. You have to stick with the program."

He grudgingly agreed, but indulgence was in his DNA. Our efforts to heal were stressful for him, which could mitigate the benefit. It was an emergency and we had to take that risk. In his wine glass, we put unsweetened cranberry juice, a little Stevia, and water. He whined the whole time, but he drank it.

By the end of filming season one, he was in great shape. In only six months, his color improved and his white cell counts were better. He had a better attitude, more energy, and he was back in fighting form to do what he loved most. J.R. Ewing was back.

During the hiatus, though, it all went to shit. I arranged for a health food store in Malibu to bring superfood smoothies and nutritious meals to his house. The deal was they'd serve him breakfast and put his lunch and dinner in the fridge to be heated up later. He swore he'd eat it all, and seemed to be sticking with the plan when I checked in with him.

But he wasn't. For most of his meals, he went out to restaurants, plus he was drinking again. The man couldn't help himself. He had to be out and about, having a party, enjoying his life. That's what made Larry Larry, even if it would also unmake him. When he came back to Dallas to film season two in September, his health was on the decline. He told us he'd been diagnosed with another cancer: acute myeloid leukemia, and had started doing intensive chemo.

Larry didn't fear death. He'd done some powerful LSD in the 1960s that gave him a unique perspective on it. As he told me many times, during that first acid trip he saw his long-dead grandmother, traversed through a tunnel of light, watched cells die and be reborn. These visions gave him the belief that there are many stages of existence, not just the one we're currently living in. He believed that death wasn't the end. He vowed back then not to worry about his eternal soul, and just have a blast in this life.

He kept his vow and didn't worry about anything, especially his health habits. He walked the edge for eighty-one years, made a party of his life, and invited everyone he knew. I felt a bit like a killjoy for him at the end, and have mixed feelings about that. But I couldn't stand by and watch Larry destroy himself. He was obviously on the way out, with cancer of the everything. We'd been friends for thirty-five years. It wasn't nearly enough. I just didn't want him to go just yet.

By Thanksgiving weekend 2012, Larry had taken a turn for the worse. He went into the hospital. Since my kids were off doing their own things, I decided to stay in Dallas for the long weekend. Patrick and his wife also stayed.

Larry, from his hospital bed, had arranged for his kids and grand-kids—all blond cuties—to come to town, take a private tour of South-fork, and be together. He had the whole weekend set up.

Patrick and I drove out to see Larry the Wednesday before the hol-iday. We walked into his room and found him sitting up in bed with his baseball cap on. It was just the three of us. Larry looked at me and said, "They gave me two weeks."

"Bullshit," I said. "We've got a scene on Monday! Plus, you just ordered a brand new Tesla and I'm going for a ride."

"Oh, I forgot about that! You're right."

We started telling some old stories, laughing and giggling. Larry seemed wonderful, with color and energy to spare. He kicked us out after two hours because his family was going to arrive soon. I kissed him and pulled his baseball hat down over his eyes. Patrick and I left. I said, "He's like a cat. He's still got a couple lives left."

For Thanksgiving, I went to my friends' home. Patrick, his wife Carlyn, and I met for coffee and dessert afterwards. We talked about Larry and what we could do. The next morning, we learned that our old friend had slipped into a coma. We rushed over to the hospital. His entire family was in the room, all of them crying. Larry was ashen and drawn. It was shocking to see him so quiet and weak. Patrick and I joined his family around the bed. Larry never came out of the coma. Even though he was eighty-one and had been in precarious health for years, his death was still a shock. Like Ed, Larry seemed to have waited for his core group of family and friends to be around him.

Patrick and I split the cast list and started making phone calls.

That was hard. I had to tell the story over and over again. Everyone was devastated by the news and I did my best to comfort them. After hanging up the last call, I broke down, sobbing, no longer needing to hold it together.

We had a beautiful memorial at Southfork. The whole while, I could swear I heard what Larry had called his celestial song, which he'd discovered while in recovery in the ICU after his 1995 liver transplant. During his post-surgery drugged-out state, he had another glimpse of the beyond, and had told me about it long ago, but it stuck in my memory. As he put it, every human has a celestial song, a hum of sorts, which is the tone of your life force. When our energy vibrates this hum, we connect to the entire universe. When he was unconscious in the ICU, he could hear his own celestial song. He recognized it, as if he'd been listening to it his entire life, and the familiarity filled him with joy. It was his belief that we all tune out our unique hum out of fear of the unknown. But if we could quiet our worries and concentrate on it, we'd feel the same bliss he did. We'd understand that our hum was just one of an infinite number of hums, which were all connected and pulsing in the celestial orchestra of energy, from one world to the next, one plane of existence to the next, one being to the next. The meaning of life, he always said, is love. So don't worry, be happy and feel good.

Please put that in your pipe and smoke it, as Mr. Hagman would have wanted. It was a bitch for him to go before we got to say goodbye, but when I picture him in his atomic bliss, grooving to the cosmic orchestra—wearing a Stetson—I just have to smile.

I kind of agree with Larry about what happens when we die, and the celestial orchestra. I don't fear death. I combat whatever anxiety I have on the subject by waking up every morning and saying "thank you" when my feet hit the floor. Death can come for any of us at any time, but I show my gratitude every morning that I've made it safely to another day.

The next thing I say is, "What am I going to do today?" I'm into living. I could worry about dying, but it's going to happen whether I worry or not. Anxiety only brings stress, which would only hasten my demise.

I expect, one day, to close my eyes and not open them again. If I leave some nuggets behind that might bring insight and joy to others, that'd be lovely. If I'm remembered with love, and that I did the best for my loved ones and the citizens of the world, that would be wonderful, too. I don't need thoughts about heaven or an afterlife to make death seem like some kind of reward. The reward is happening right now, on Earth, as we live and love every day. I'll second Larry's fear-free sentiment: The meaning of life is love. So don't worry. Be happy. Feel good.

SHED

We filmed the *Dallas 2.0* season three finale in April 2014, and soon after were informed that there'd been a change in the hierarchy at TNT, our network. The new regime came in and they weren't sure about bringing *Dallas* back for season four.

Dugie and I returned to our home in California to sit and stew for a while. Since I was under contract, I wasn't free to take other work until a decision was made. None of us could. The entire cast and crew waited on tenterhooks for six months with no income, our frustration and feeling of helplessness growing by the day. Finally, in October, strangers called and summarily fired us all.

We'd become a family, and the network overlords tore us apart. That was the sad part. Otherwise, I was furious. How could the network treat us so disrespectfully and deny us the chance to take other jobs for six months? They'd unfairly left us, and our fans, hanging. I get it, when new management comes in they clean the slate. But we'd left so many storylines open at the end of season three, so many unanswered questions. The cast lobbied the network to bring us back for one more season to wrap it all up. We got over 1,000,000 tweets under the #savedallas hashtag, but it didn't seem to matter to TNT. We were done.

Along with my ire, I was left with a practical problem. I had a condo's worth of stuff in Dallas to deal with. I cooked most of my own meals and had outfitted the kitchen. Between Dallas and Los Angeles, I now had two of everything. Two garlic presses, two coffee grinders, two blenders. The idea of packing up the condo was too loathsome, so I just kept paying rent, hoping the show would miraculously get rescued from the jaws of defeat by another network. After another few months, I accepted that that was not going to happen.

I already had a storage unit full of old furniture and the attic in my guesthouse was bursting with boxes of stuff. My garage was too packed to get my car in. I'd been living in the same house for forty years and never had the opportunity to do a major purge. I didn't get rid of stuff, I just got more of it, including thirty crates of financial records that had been sent over by my accountant. He'd decided to fire all his clients that fell below a certain income threshold. I didn't make the cut.

I arranged for everything in Dallas to be packed and shipped to L.A., and crammed it all into my guest bedroom. Boxes from floor to ceiling. The idea of dealing with it was just too daunting. I just shut the door and ignored it.

Soon after, I was working in the garden, wondering where the hell I was going to do with a lifetime of accumulated stuff, and the word *shed* popped into my head. I did have a large shed that was currently full of tools, dirt, and chopped firewood. Maybe I could shove the Dallas condo stuff in there, and move the financial records out of the storage unit and into the garage, and move the boxes of junk in the garage into the attic . . .

And then my subconscious kicked me in the ass and said, "Not shed. *Shed.*" The answer to my accumulation problem was to *shed* the stuff like a useless dead skin. I would make like a snake and sell or donate *everything* in the Dallas house. What I couldn't shed, like all

those financial records, I'd shred. I didn't need it. I didn't want it. I'd
get rid of it. The idea of shedding stored stuff felt so good, I ran around
my house and everywhere I looked, I found something that I couldn't
wait to get rid of.

In your 20s and 30s, it's all about aspiration. You dream big and fanta-
size about the things and memories you'll one day have. In your 40s,
50s, and 60s, you accumulate and fill your life with possessions that
reinforce your status and remind you of your accomplishments. When
you get to your 70s, life is about assessment. You look at every object,
emotion, and relationship and ask, "Do I really need this?" If the answer is "no," you can't get rid of it fast enough. It's not that you're too
old and feeble to carry around all the stuff. You just don't see the point
of hauling great piles of shit around anymore. It's dead weight.

I started making lists on my yellow legal pad of places to clean out
and things that I'd accumulated over a lifetime. The list got impossibly
long, so I threw it to the side and just got busy.

I went immediately to my closet, which had hundreds of things
I'd worn once—pants that no longer fit, shirts I hated when I bought
them in 1995, outfits that were trendy in 1987. I started pulling them
out. The pile on the bed got higher and higher. I donated all of it to
the Anne Douglas Center in L.A., founded by Anne and Kirk Douglas
to help women at risk who needed new clothes to start their lives over.
Well, maybe someone would walk around in shoulder pad blouses and
designer overalls.

I also came upon a small box of jewelry, a couple of emerald and
diamond cocktail rings that my father convinced me to buy forty years
ago when he found them at an estate sale. I purchased them in the
'80s as investment objects with no intention of wearing the gaudy
things, and never did. Nor could I imagine wearing them now. Trying
them on, I was reminded of my Dad, dead now for twenty-five years,
and how he urged me to make the purchase in case I ever needed
money one day. I thought about giving the rings to Kehly. And then

I thought of selling them, selling all of my "real" jewelry, small collection though it was, and traveling the world, or throwing a huge party, in Italy maybe. The rings never gave me joy, but just the thought of selling them put a huge smile on my face. (I haven't done it yet; it's on my To Do list.)

I emptied my garage over a period of weeks. I cleaned out the room in my guesthouse full of denim teddy bears (don't ask), and hired someone to come shred all those ancient financial records.

But that was just the beginning. Objects were easy to clear away. The real test of shedding would be dropping the thousand pounds of useless emotions I'd amassed as well, starting with how angry I was when *Dallas* got canceled.

I wallowed for months. Along with anger and resentment about being canceled, I felt doubt about my future, fear about finding another job. But a few months of wallowing was long enough. Yes, it was unfair to the fans. It was wrong for them to keep us waiting for a "no." But now it was time to get over it and move on.

I'd bounced back from defeat many times before. I called it the Trampoline Effect, when I'd bounce high in victory and then sink low in defeat, only to rebound again by sheer determination. I'd done it before; I could do it now; I'd probably do it again. I told myself, "Shed the anger. Shed the resentment. Something better and magical will come along." Later that same week, I got the call about coming to London to play the Fairy Godmother in *Cinderella*. I was right. Something magical—with a wand and tiara—did come along.

As I purged my house and my mind of things, emotions, and ideas I didn't need, I realized I had something else to shed as well. We all wear masks, a false face, with certain people and in certain circumstances. My mask was the People Pleaser. I'd been wearing it since I was a child, the good girl, the responsible daughter, the accommodating wife, the worker bee, the woman who hated letting anyone down.

Was I really such a people pleaser underneath it all? If I threw the mask away, I could resolve to please myself. It's not that I wanted to turn into a selfish narcissist. I just wanted to be 100 percent honest. It's such an important goal, to know yourself, and to shed the way you and other people, have defined you for years and years. How many of us can really stand up and say, "This is who I am"? I strive for complete authenticity in my every word, deed, and decision. It's not so easy to dig deep and understand who you really are without masks and labels to guide you.

I would define myself as a person who knows what's truly valuable in this world. And it's not a guest room full of redundant kitchen objects.

All of it had to go. Just as you can choose to be happy and choose to pursue joy, you can choose to face your fears and absolve yourself of guilt. Regret is beyond me at this point. Most of the people I've offended were dead or forgave me years ago. As for doubt, I've proven myself to myself many times over. I didn't have to prove myself to anyone else.

The more I thought about it, *shed* was the one word that encompassed everything I wanted to do with the rest of my life, to clear out the tired and old, and make way for the exciting and new.

To feel young and alive you have to put yourself in the frame of mind of having nothing but bright ideas for your fabulous, unencumbered future. Old patterns (of behavior, of china) are rubbish and need to be trashed. Assess, "Do I really need this?" about grudges, attitudes, labels, and masks. Assess, "Do I really need this?" about self-pity, anger, hang-ups, bad habits, and prejudices.

Everything negative, useless, and redundant *must go.*

This might've been a long, roundabout way of asking, dear Readers, do you happen to be in need of a garlic press, a coffee grinder, or a blender? Only three years old! Good quality stuff! I'm giving it away.

SUIT UP WITH
STYLE

You know those "How to Dress Your Age" articles that run in fashion magazines? Notice how they usually cover women in their "20s, 30s, 40s, and Beyond!" If women abided by the "and Beyond" rules of age-appropriate style, we'd be stuck wearing pantsuits, caftans, cardigans, and boxy jackets from sixty until death. Even sadder than age-appropriate? Ageless. Ageless is code for classic and classic is code for boring. Unless buttoned-up and black genuinely fills your heart with joy, ageless is a trap.

Let women in their 20s, 30s, and 40s worry about rules. When you stop dressing for any purpose or person other than your own amusement, style gets interesting. I don't think younger women can do it. They're too caught up in dressing to impress. Wise people don't bother with such superficial concerns. Whether we're in a gown or grungy sweats, we dress to express the ebullience of being alive.

The following fashion nuggets have been inspired by my own

adventures in shopping for, wearing, and recycling clothes. I've also lifted ideas from fashion icons, the real deals, women who have devoted their lives to looking sharp.

Fashion Nugget #1: Show Off Your Goods

"Delete the negative; accentuate the positive."
—*Donna Karan*

In your youth, you probably did the hard, humbling work of figuring out how to dress for your body type. If you're big on the bottom, wear A-line skirts and clingy tops. If you've got no waist, a pencil skirt plus a V-neck top, etc. We have had a lifetime of trial and error regarding the mechanics of getting dressed. We know which cuts flatter our shape and which colors warm our skin tone. So when it comes to deleting the negative and accentuating the positive, we aren't talking about Fashion 101 tricks like how to camouflage a belly pouch or create the illusion of a long leg.

Fashion negative to get rid of: Fear. Of patterns, fabrics, colors, making a statement, being risqué, dressing dangerously. I've been shopping with friends and suggested one try on a red leather moto jacket. It was like I'd asked her to kill someone. "No! I could never! How could you suggest such a thing?" Okay, so maybe red leather isn't right for her. But how could she know, if she refused to try it on? Look, women, we've survived countless trials and traumas. We've worked hard for decades at jobs that challenged us, as parents to kids who drove us crazy, at marriages that weren't easy. We've buried parents, friends, husbands. Some of us have buried children. We have been to the wars and survived. We don't need to be afraid of a jacket anymore.

Fashion positives to accentuate: The joy in your heart via bold patterns and bright colors. Your hard-won softness around the edges via luxurious fabrics that feel yummy against your skin. Your confidence by wearing kick-ass boots or a piece of statement jewelry. Your intelligence by combining pin stripes and plaid. Your flexibility in finding fifteen uses for one red belt. Show who you are in what you wear. Express the finest parts of personality through fashion, and you'll share these gifts with the world whenever you leave your house.

Fashion Nugget #2: Trends Are for Amateurs

"I never wanted to look young. I wanted to look *great.*"
—Joyce Carpati

I've never met Joyce, eighty, a former fashion editor at *Cosmo*, but I feel like I know her, having watched her sing and dress beautifully in the documentary *Advanced Style*. The inspiring movie (and the blog, and the book, and the coloring book) was the passion project of Ari Seth Cohen, a thirtysomething photographer who roams the streets of New York City, taking pictures of fifty-plus-year-old women with fabulous fashion sense. He was inspired and awed by his stylish grandmothers as a boy. As an adult, he was mystified that no one in the fashion universe paid attention to this dynamic subset of the population. "In America, once you turn a certain age, you're sort of forgotten, you're sort of made to feel that you're invisible," Cohen told the *New York Times* in 2011. "What I'm trying to do is give these women a voice and also show people that your life doesn't end at fifty." The women he admires "are confident," he said to the interviewer. "They know what they like, they know what suits their bodies, and they're dressing for themselves. They don't dress based on trends."

I sure did, for a long time and I've got the shoulder pads and pleated white trousers and suspenders to prove it. When I stopped paying any attention to trends, that's when I found my own true style—classic with an edge—that gives me the most confidence and comfort. Stepping away from trends made me realize that following them makes you invisible. If everyone is wearing the same thing, you don't stand out. Following trends is the opposite of expressing your individuality. I don't expect every woman to go out there and blaze dynamic trails like the ladies in *Advanced Style* (a must watch; streaming on Netflix). We're not all going to rock a feather boa or turban. But we can all put our unique stamp on an outfit and make any outfit our own.

Fashion Nugget #3: Wear Your Clothes, Don't Let Them Wear You

"Confidence. If you have it, you can make anything
look good."
—Diane von Furstenberg

If some designer happens to send me a piece of clothing, I'm more than happy to wear it. But for the most part, I wear a uniform. Not an actual uniform, like I wore in Catholic school. I mean my go-to outfits, the ones that are comfortable, reliable, look great, feel good, and fit well. I have my uniforms for just about every scenario in life. My Dinner Out uni, Party uni, Movie Date uni, Talk Show uni, and so on. I've got multiple choices for each scenario, but they're pretty much the same with slight variations. It's taken me a long time to build a closet full of comfortable choices. I know whatever I pull out will work.

The extra bit of flare I add to my uniform? The equivalent of a big, bold broach? It's the knowledge that my natural personality will shine through. I wear my clothes; they don't wear me. When we go out to dinner, you'll remember that I looked pretty and was well dressed. You'll remember my smile and bits of our conversation. But you might not remember exactly what I had on. Even if I spent a lot of time getting dressed, this is my goal. I want people to remember me, not my clothes, to look at me, not the fifteen accessories I've got on. When you have to dig deep under piles of jewelry and makeup and labels to find the woman, you have to wonder, *What is she hiding?*

Confidence means not using your clothes to camouflage yourself. It's one thing to have fun with fashion and quite another to hide behind it.

Fashion Nugget #4: Shed All Labels

"Fashion is what you are offered four times a year by designers. And style is what you choose."
—*Lauren Hutton*

Some fashion people are obsessed. Friends of mine read a dozen fashion blogs and talk about designers like personal friends (they're not). They go shopping every week just to see the new arrivals. They check out every woman's outfit as she comes through the door, running down her clothes, telling me price tags and label names. I won't go to a restaurant with these fashionistas anymore. Are they having lunch with me or gawking at strangers? It's a bit insulting.

As I said, I enjoy shopping and I love great clothes . . . to a point. I will not spend thousands on a dress. I'm very practical about what I can afford and what my priorities are. Spending the cost equivalent of a long weekend in Hawaii on one dress? That will never appear on my priorities list.

In the last chapter, I talked about shedding the labels we give ourselves, or that others have bestowed upon us. But I also believe in shedding attachment and obsession with designer labels, too. Our consumerist culture has created a toxic, envious environment where people judge each other's worth based on who they're wearing. You could have on the ugliest, most unflattering piece of crap, but if the right name is stitched into the label, you'll be admired for it by shallow, status-seekers who, unfortunately, are often the loudest people in the room. Conversely, you could be wearing a well-made and adorable dress you dug out of your closet, and some people will look down on you for it. How do I know this? It happens to me. I've shown up at parties and dinners, and been asked point blank, "Wherever did you find that dress?"

"It's vintage!" I say, and leave it at that. I know I look good. If they judge me, that is their problem.

Fashion can be a distraction and an addiction like drugs, alcohol, gambling, the Internet. Obsessing about beautiful clothes might be a way to avoid thinking about less flattering emotions. When my friend goes off on some woman for wearing a subpar label (in her opinion), I always think, *What is wrong with you? What aren't you getting in your life? Why are you so angry?*

Fashion exists to make money for the clothing industry. Great style, on the other hand, is how you live your life, treat your friends, and incorporate beauty and kindness into your being every day, regardless of what you wear.

SHOW YOURSELF

In 2001 my manager and I were chatting, and she mentioned that Morgan Fairchild had been offered the part of Mrs. Robinson in a production of *The Graduate* in London.

I said, "Good for Morgan." Performing on Broadway and the West End was any actor's dream, presenting the ultimate challenge. "I would love to do that part." I'd felt an affinity for Mrs. Robinson ever since my leg was Anne Bancroft's stunt double on the movie poster back in the '60s.

My manager seemed surprised by my interest. For one thing, Mrs. Robinson appeared nude onstage in what had to be the longest scene in dramatic history (fifiteen seconds), at least for the actor playing her. I hadn't done so much as a wet T-shirt contest. I had trouble walking around naked in front of one person, let alone a crowd of thousands. But as an actor, I was up for any creative challenge.

When Morgan decided against doing it, I asked my manager to put my name forward.

The producers said, "Linda Gray is too old." Mrs. Robinson was supposed to be in her forties. I was sixty at the time.

"Too old for what?" I replied. Not too old to tread the boards in my birthday suit, if that was what they were afraid of. I sent over some recent photographs to show them what I looked like.

My manager and the producers went back and forth and in the end, they offered me the part. As soon as they did, though, I had second thoughts. Theoretical tasteful nudity was quite a different animal than goosefleshed, actual butt nakedness. I called a friend in London and asked her to go check out Kathleen Turner, who was in the role at the time, and tell me how exposed she was up there. "It's discreet," she reported back. The lighting came through shutters that obscured all of Ms. Turner's bits. Wavering still, I called Maj Hagman for a kick in the pants. She said, "Don't even think about it. Get on a plane and get your bare ass up on that stage!"

By the time my run started, I would be the fifth Mrs. Robinson, after Kathleen Turner, forty-five; Jerry Hall, forty-three; Amanda Donahue, thirty-nine; and Anne Archer, fifty-three. The cast and crew were icy to me when I arrived, as if they were expecting me to behave like a Hollywood Diva. I suspected that my predecessors might've benefited from a Dale Carnegie course in treating others with respect. To change the cast's assumptions about me, I worked hard and was friendly from the get-go. Bette Davis would *not* have approved of how solicitous and easygoing I was, but my strategy worked. Their British stiff upper lips melted and before long, we were a jolly crew.

The Gielgud Theatre wasn't the most lavish, but I loved it. I was assigned the Vanessa Redgrave dressing room; just knowing she had used it once gave me a little thrill. It was a charming little room with a couch and dressing table, and a little box of poison in the corner kept away the rats.

I'd been struggling with the nude scene in dress rehearsals. I just couldn't bring myself to drop the towel. The director was patient with me, but at the last dress, he gently insisted I let it go. The lighting expert needed to get the shutter effect in the right places. I walked out on stage and stood on my mark. I took a deep breath, dropped the towel, and absolutely *froze*. Across my body, slats of light and dark appeared and were adjusted. After a few minutes, I was allowed to pick up the towel. I grabbed it and ran backstage, down the stairs, and into the Vanessa Redgrave dressing room, where I hid behind the couch.

A day later, I was sitting at my vanity table, putting on my Mrs. Robinson wig, when one of the stagehands burst into my dressing room, clearly upset.

He said, "Ms. Gray, I am so sorry."

I thought of my family. "What's wrong?" He wouldn't speak. I said, "My God, just tell me!"

"Come upstairs."

He brought me into an office with a television. On the screen, chaos, mayhem, screams of sirens, clouds of dust. I had no idea what I was looking at. The news crawl at the bottom of the screen said there'd been a terrorist attack in New York City, and that the Twin Towers had collapsed, killing thousands. A picture of the Pentagon came on, pouring smoke. A plane wreck in Pennsylvania. Devastation in lower Manhattan. Fifteen people were crammed into the office to watch the telly. I was the only American among them.

My colleagues were wonderfully supportive and offered me whatever help I needed. But they couldn't put me on a plane or teleport me the 7,000 miles back to my home, my family, my country where I belonged. We watched and talked, all of us stunned.

After an hour, I left the theater and went back to my hotel. A bunch of American tourists were in the lobby, drinking and commiserating. But that felt wrong, too. I didn't want to talk to anyone, countrymen or otherwise, except family. I tried to reach the kids, but couldn't get through.

Alone in my room, I stayed up all night, crying, stricken with grief and fear, riveted to the TV and wishing I were home. I'd never felt more alone in my life.

The next day, the whole world woke up into a scarier new reality where people flew planes into buildings and no one felt safe. It was also my sixty-first birthday.

We were scheduled to open that day. Thousands of tickets had been sold, many to American tourists on holiday. In light of recent events, however, we had no idea if anyone would come. But at show time, we opened our doors and the house filled up. Despite the real possibility of a terrorist attack in London (it would come in 2005 when four bombs were exploded simultaneously on the Underground, killing fifty-two and injuring over 700), people refused to cower in their hotel rooms and flats. They would risk their safety to see us. In my case, to see *all* of me.

Dropping the towel was the least I could do.

Nothing like a tragedy of global proportion to put a little nudity into perspective.

Oh, I continued to be traumatized by dropping that towel, from opening night until the show closed four months later. It never got easier to expose myself. The first week, someone in the audience snapped a photo of me in my all together. The grainy—but not nearly grainy enough—picture was all over the papers the next day. You'd think that a naked grandmother wouldn't be front-page news the week of 9/11. One of the tabloids ran a photo display of all the previous Mrs. Robinsons and me, criticizing our bodies and judging me, the oldest, the "winner." I would have been flattered if I weren't disgusted and embarrassed.

That week, every American reacted to the terrorist attacks on our soil by feeling exposed, raw, and vulnerable. I had the same emotional reaction, compounded by being literally exposed, raw, and vulnerable onstage every night of the week, twice on Wednesdays and Saturdays.

But I stayed calm and carried on. The show went on, too, as did all of us after the attacks on 9/11. When being brave is the only choice you have, you make it.

During that time, I began reading *The Artist's Way* by Julia

Cameron. As Cameron prescribed, I started writing "morning pages" every day and loved the experience of jotting down whatever came into my mind. No spelling or punctuation was necessary, just a free-flowing stream of consciousness. Cameron also encouraged going on dates with yourself to simply wander wherever your heart took you to, museums, galleries, fabric shops, the kinds of places you wouldn't take the time to visit if you weren't on a play date with yourself. Just getting lost was exciting. When I travel, I usually put on my walking shoes and trot around the city I'm visiting just to acquaint myself with its rhythm, check out where the locals go for their coffee in the morning, listen to their accents.

During the run of *The Graduate*, including the days right after 9/11, I kept up with my morning walks. I remember choosing to make the start of each day beautiful. I would get a cappuccino at the local coffee bar, walk across Piccadilly, sit on a park bench, and comment on how well the gardeners did that day. In the light of the terrorist attacks, such simple pleasures might seem silly and frivolous. But did I care? Nope! Did they make me happy? Yep! I'd even say those morning walks gave me strength to reveal myself.

I chose to take the part and I chose to drop the towel. No one yanked it away from me. I put myself willingly in a situation that would cause powerful negative emotions, including embarrassment, shame, and fear. As an actor, you learn early on that if you're comfortable, you're not getting anywhere. Creativity is found in those dark nooks and uncomfortable crannies. Creativity takes courage.

It's a natural tendency to want to avoid the powerfully uncomfortable. But if we cut ourselves off from that end of the emotional spectrum, then we'll inadvertently lop off the cozy end as well. Unless we're willing to expose our authentic selves (if not our naked flesh) to each other—especially in hard times—we won't make the genuine connections that are the ultimate source of joy for us. Navigating through shameful, embarrassing, painful situations with honesty and courage are what give us a sense of self-worth. By being vulnerable, afraid and sharing ourselves anyway, we make ourselves worthy of love.

Remember the weeks after 9/11, how in our fear and vulnerability, we came together as a nation? When I took my clothes off and felt completely exposed, I was shored up by the audience, and the cast, and crew. They were on my side, and their support got me through it and enriched the entire experience for all of us.

You might not find yourself stripped on a stage, but the metaphor is only too apt for dozens of deeply personal, terrifying experiences. In a paper gown in a hospital bed in front of a doctor with a clipboard and cold hands. In a conference room chair at a lawyer's office. Facing a boss when applying for a job. Sitting opposite a potential lover on a date.

We're all in showbiz. The show, wherever it is, must go on. Even if we get our bare, quivering, spotty asses handed to us, just giving it your all strengthens your feelings of self-worth. Every day, every scene, is an opportunity to drop the towel, show yourself, and be loved for it.

TRAVEL LIGHT

I've lived in my house for forty years now. Ed and I built it piece by piece, from the floors to the rafters. We put in the pool, and the barn, the tennis court. When Ed's parents got older, we built the guesthouse with a kitchenette, so they could be comfortable when they visited us. We put in the Jacuzzi last. I've redecorated a few times since our divorce, just to make the place my own. The house is full of memories of raising my kids, holidays, parties, quiet days by the pool, and starry nights. We took a vacant lot and turned it into a magical oasis that nurtures my soul.

I think about selling it every day.

It's not that I don't love my house. I do. But lately, it's become this heavy weight, what's keeping me stuck in one place while my spirit yearns to float free.

House maintenance is tough. I keep writing enormous checks to repair the air conditioning or the septic system. I'm not even here a lot of the time. Of the last twelve months, I lived in this house for only four of them.

My friends have often asked me why I don't sell and move to the city. I'm inching closer. Something will tap me on the shoulder and let me know the right time to move. If someone drove by, fell in love with the place, and made me a decent offer on the spot, I'd probably take it.

A couple of years ago, a fireman pulled into my driveway. My first thought? *Stripper gram?* Sadly, no. The fireman told me that a wildfire was closing in, and I had one hour to evacuate. At the time, Jeff was staying in the guesthouse. We both had cats. I called him to come home right away, but he was on a marathon bike ride, well over an hour away. "Just throw what you can into the car," he said. "I'll get there as soon as I can."

With the help of my son-in-law, I corralled both cats into carriers and filled every suitcase I had in a packing frenzy, grabbed our laptops, and burned rubber getting out of there. Lance wanted me to go to their house, but they had dogs and no room for Jeff, me, and the cats. So I started calling around for a room.

For miles in every direction, the hotels were full. I finally found a roadside motel sixty miles away that had one room with twin beds. Jeff met me there and the two of us lived like Beverly Hillbillies, our tiny box room crammed with over-packed suitcases, containing everything and yet nothing useful. I'd been so quick to save photographs and financial papers, I didn't pack any underwear or pajamas. The cats hated each other and each staked out a space under a bed to hiss and spit in the other's general direction. We made an impromptu cat pan by cutting the top off a box of litter. For four days, we had to head off the motel owner with his strict "no pets" policy. Whenever he walked by, Jeff and I start hissing and spitting at each other to cover the cats. Our room was on the end of a row, with the ice machine right outside our door. Every ten minutes, twenty-four hours a day, it made a crunching sound.

We were there for four days. Four days of trying to keep the cats quiet and fed. Four days of listening to that damn ice machine crunching. Four days in the same clothes. Four days of eating greasy food at the nearby diner. Four of the funniest, most hilarious, laugh-filled days of my life.

Jeff and I didn't stop laughing, even though the fires raged in the Canyon and our cats wanted to tear each other's faces off. We laughed harder as our clothes got so filthy, they ripened. The food really was atrocious but we made fast friends with the truckers and the people who ran the place. Since we had three meals a day there, it would have been impossible not to. They let us use their garbage to throw out our empty cat food tins.

We did sneak back to the house a few times. The whole area was cordoned off, guarded by firemen. We drove over and basically begged to be let through the barriers to feed the koi. At first, the firemen wouldn't allow it. "They're twenty years old," I pleaded. "They'll die!" One fireman took pity on me and led me through the neighborhood one morning. It was eerily silent. We felt like thieves, stealing into our own property. After I fed the fish, the fireman made us leave. I didn't get to go inside, but the house was still standing. When we got the news that we could return, I was sad that our adventure was over.

What would you pack if you were given one hour to evacuate your house?

It's a dinner party conversation topic. Experts say to grab your financial records, computer, passport, photo albums, and wallet. It's certainly wise to be logical and take the things you can't easily replace. I packed all that, but none of it really mattered. I was given the gift of a forced evacuation and learned in a hurry what was really important to me:

Kids and cats.

I've been saying this all along . . .

It was liberating to know that I could live without everything inside my house, as well as the house itself. I could wear yoga pants for four days and laugh so hard with my son. I started to wonder: What would life be like if I packed a few suitcases (with underwear and PJs), threw them in my car, and drove away? It's Advanced Shedding. What you're getting rid of isn't only the brick-and-mortar structure that is the home base of your life. It's the very idea that you have to have a home base. We get so attached to our four walls and a roof, and equate it with security. But the truth is, your place in the world is secured by the people in it.

If my house did burn in a wildfire, I'd be inconvenienced for a while. I'd have to deal with a shit ton of paperwork. But I would not rebuild. I'd take the insurance money and roam.

I've learned to travel light. One day a few years back, I was preparing to go to Rome and Paris for ten days. Patrick Duffy and I were invited to appear on an Italian TV show. Since the trip was close to our shared birthday, I invited Ryder, my grandson, then seventeen, to come along.

My friend Barbara Pizik came by as I was preparing to leave. She said, "You could do the entire trip with only a carry-on."

I laughed at the concept.

She said, "Watch how it's done."

Barbara proceeded to pull things out of my closet, mix them with scarves, jewelry, and only one jacket that would carry me through ten days of travel. It could work. If we all packed just a carry-on our trip would be so much easier.

Next, I had to convince Mr. Duffy. He said, "I have a tux. I can't do carry-on." I countered that I had a long dress, plus heels, plus jewelry, and street clothes.

Ryder balked at the idea, too. "I have so many shirts, I'll never be able to fit them in a carry-on."

I informed both of them that I wasn't going to wait for them go get their checked luggage. It took too much time. Reluctantly, they agreed to try carry-on, although I'm sure there were words sent quietly to me under their breath.

Off we went to Rome. The three of us wheeled our cases through the airports and I smiled smugly. I'm proud to say that Patrick now only travels with a carry-on. He even irons his own shirts when he gets to his hotel. What a guy!

After Rome, Patrick went home and Ryder and I went to Paris. We spent the next five days there, trotting all over the city. He loved french fries and I told him, "You're in the land of french fries!" I introduced him to *entrecote* (French-cut steak) with fries, *moules frittes* (mussels with fries), and chocolate croissants and cappuccinos for breakfast every morning. What a divine and delicious time we had.

We didn't think about the clothes we were wearing. We were totally focused on having fun, seeing and feeling the magic of Paris together. I don't think he even noticed that I wore the same brown leather jacket every day. Did it matter? Not in the least.

I've used only carry-ons ever since, and love the freedom plus the creativity of using only what I have to look a little different every day. If not, does it really matter if I don't? Traveling with someone you love and focusing on fun and food beats having a perfectly matched outfit any day.

SHUSH ✶

When you get to be my age, certain subjects are off limits. I don't have the time or the inclination to waste one minute talking about nonsense. If you bring up these topics, I will tune you out or might have to tell you, with all the love in the world, to please be quiet about . . .

HOW FAT YOU ARE. How many of us have been trying to lose ten pounds (or more) for twenty years (or more)? If we could shed the obsession with fat and wrinkles, we'd have so much more time, thought, and energy to . . . I don't know, learn piano or plant a garden or read a book. Staring into space for hours would be a huge improvement over saying, "I hate my [fill in the body parts]." Carping about your weight only calls attention to it in your mind and the person you're whining to. I would so much rather talk about how sexy you are, what healthy food you're eating, the long walk you took today, and how pretty you look in that dress.

HOW OLD YOU FEEL. As soon as you say, "I'm so old!" you have put one of your withered feet in your grave. I'd never say such a thing, nor dwell on it. I'd much rather discuss ways to feel alive and young, things to do to get the heart pumping, ideas for putting a spring in your step. You're only as old as you tell other people you feel. By forcing them to listen to it, you're rapidly aging them as well.

PETTY DRAMAS. I have friends who call to describe, in agonizing detail, every slightly contentious conversation with the dry cleaner or their husbands, as if I give a shit. My head isn't an empty bin to be filled with their sagas. I've got plenty of my own thoughts to occupy my mental space. If you notice that I have stopped taking your calls or cut off conversations in mid-sentence, please take the hint.

COMPLAINING. The traffic was bad. The line was long. The strawberries had mold. Complaining is how people transfer their annoyance and frustration onto someone else. It's a selfish act. If you simply must complain about life's little stressors, tell the sky. Tell the trees. Write about them in the world's most tedious diary. But please spare the rest of humanity. We have our own stress to deal with.

BLAMING. I don't care who's responsible for the injustices in your world. Assigning blame doesn't solve the problem. Instead, let's talk about solutions.

CRITICISMS. Even worse than complaining about yourself is criticizing others. If I have to listen to one more conversation about so-and-so's botched plastic surgery, or how fat someone got, or how old, I am going to scream. You can make the conscious choice never to criticize anyone again, be she a stranger, a friend, or yourself. A confident person does not need to build herself up by trashing someone else. I'd always rather talk about and look for the positive things, or examine a situation for the deeper meaning. Let's talk about why women feel they have to have surgery, instead of trashing someone for getting her eyes done.

BRAGGING. Don't tell me how much money you made, or how you beat out five other people for a job, or how much weight you lost, or how many words you wrote today (especially annoying to hear from my author pals as I write this book). Bragging robs your friends of the opportunity of congratulating you on your accomplishments. Please share the good news, but don't gild the lily. The only exception: Brag away about your kids and grandkids—and then listen to me do the same.

OTHER PEOPLE'S ILLNESSES. When you cross sixty-five, a lot of conversations center on the various conditions and diseases of friends and acquaintances. It's one thing to give a health update to interested parties, but it's quite another to troll for the gruesome details about another person's suffering. It translates as, "Thank God it's not me." One day it will be you, and you wouldn't like it if your illness becomes fodder. You don't make yourself healthier by gossiping about the illness of others.

THE BEST WAY TO DIE. A popular dinner party conversation topic when you're a teenager. It gets a lot less fun when you cross sixty and people in your life start to die in unexpected, horrible ways. Go ahead and plan your death. God will laugh. I'll be tuning you out and planning my life.

UNREALIZED DREAMS. I'm sorry you never ran a marathon or wrote your novel. I'm sorry you never got married, had kids, made a million dollars, or whatever dream you once had that didn't come true. Instead of moaning about what went wrong, shed the old dreams and clean the slate for some new, realistic ones.

UNMET EXPECTATIONS. When people say, "Is that all there is?" they define their lives by disappointment. We've all felt it, about big and small matters. But then you have to pick yourself back up, celebrate the effort you made, and try again to exceed expectations the next time around. In Peggy Lee's classic tune about disillusionment, she sang, "Is that all there is? Is that all there is? If that's all there is my friends, then let's keep dancing. Let's break out the booze and have a ball. If that's all there is." Yes, let's keep dancing, let's have a ball, because loving life and enjoying each other *is* all there is.

OVERCOMING THE
OBSTACLES IN YOUR PATH

Before I'd heard about the Brazilian healer John of God (henceforth JoG) through the years from a bunch of sources—friends, documentaries, articles, the woowoo pipeline I was plugged into. When I received a scary diagnosis in 2012—clamping of the retinal arteries due to high blood pressure—and was told that Western medicine could not cure the impaired vision in my right eye, a group of believers from Dallas who I think of as my metaphysical family urged me to join them on their annual journey to Brazil at JoG's "spiritual hospital." Their plan was to arrive in late December and stay for two weeks. I was never a big fan of New Year's and would be glad to miss it at home, but I had to be back in Dallas January 7 for filming. A week seemed like enough time, so I booked my flight.

I packed all my whites (required dress code; your aura stood out more clearly in while, apparently), and went to the airport, excited for my first visit to South America. The check-in counter woman took my passport and said, "You can't go to Brazil. You don't have a visa."

I needed a visa? News to me. I nervously called the travel agent who had made all of the arrangements and left a voicemail. She was traveling, too. I said to the check-in woman, "Where do I get a visa?" thinking I could buy one at an airport kiosk.

"You have to apply and it takes seventy-two hours."

There was nothing I could do at the moment, so I took a deep breath and went back to my condo in Dallas to investigate. I reached one of my metaphysical family members. She texted, "Forgot to tell you. We all have ten-year visas. Sorry!"

Great.

It was Saturday night and the only agency open on Sunday was an hour from my condo. Miraculously, someone answered the phone and agreed to see me the next day at noon. I made the drive, but came up empty. Despite being well-organized and friendly, the clerk gave me the same story: I had to wait seventy-two hours for a visa, *after* I applied on Monday, the next business day.

I was not discouraged by the rigmarole. In a way, I'd expected it. One of my friends had told me that obstacles were put in your path, like a pre-screening test of your commitment and worthiness, whenever you decided to meet JoG. Part of me wanted to stay home, read a book, get caught up on *Breaking Bad* and *Mad Men*. But something deep inside said, "Don't give up. You will get there and it'll be glorious."

My next idea was to get on any plane in the right direction. Which country was a neighbor of Brazil's and doesn't require a visa? *Buenas noches, Argentina.* I booked a New Year's Eve overnight flight to Buenos Aires. The flight attendant gave me a bottle of champagne to take with me since I had slept through midnight. My travel agent surfaced, found a hotel room for me there, and paid for it herself to apologize for screwing up the visa thing.

The Buenos Aires leg of the schlep was a pleasure. But the concierge at my hotel there sang me the same sad song, that I'd have to wait seventy-two hours to get into Brazil, earliest, but probably longer, since today was New Year's and nothing would be open. He predicted I wouldn't get to Brazil until January 5, one day before I had to turn around and leave. Not acceptable. The nearest place I could hope to get a visa sooner was the remote town of Iguazu Falls. Seeing my determination, the concierge arranged my flight and helped me book a hotel room in that border town for the next day. I gave him a nice tip and the bottle of champagne I'd been given at New Year's on the plane.

For dinner that night, I had an Argentinian steak with red wine, quite a meal for a mostly vegetarian eater. I needed the protein for the next day of begging at a foreign office with very limited Spanish. On January 2 I took a puddle-jumper to Iguazu Falls, and a taxi to the visa office. My English-speaking driver was a tremendous help and waited with me on the line to speak to the clerk in the window about my options. I handed him my passport and said, "*Deseo una visa para Brazil hoy, por favor.*" (That was it for my Spanish.)

He said, "Twenty-four hours."

"No, *hoy!*" Today! I smiled and used eye contact.

We went back and forth a few times with my driver translating. The line got longer behind me. Finally, the clerk told me to have a seat and wait. I took this as a good sign. My translator/driver left and the waiting area quickly filled up with other people, an international smattering that included a Japanese family, a couple from Australia, an Austrian and his Swedish wife, all of us hoping for visas that day. After four hours and some lively conversation with new friends from around the world, the clerk issued all of us ten-day visas to Brazil. We gave each other hugs and high fives. Victory!

As soon as possible, I booked a ticket to Brasilia. Before my evening flight, I sent texts to all the people who'd helped me along the way, the travel agent and the clerk back in Texas, the concierge in Buenos Aires, my friends already at the Casa de Dom Inácio de Loyola (JoG's compound). They were all duly impressed by my progress. I was inching closer, and would arrive at my original destination later than expected, but in time for JoG's office hours. He only saw patients on Wednesday through Friday. I'd swing into town on Thursday evening, wake up Friday, and have my procedure, or whatever it was he would do.

After landing in Brasilia, I still had to travel eighty miles to the town of Abadiania. It was dark already and my cell phone was dead. I asked the taxi drivers lined up at the airport, "English?"

They all shook their heads. I held up my phone and asked, "Charger?" making the international symbol of plugging something in. One driver nodded yes. I handed him the address, hooked up my phone, and settled in for a one-and-a-half-hour drive in silence.

Fifteen minutes along the way, the cabbie said, "Emergency stop." I thought maybe something was wrong with the car. He pulled off to the side of the road. Another car pulled up right next to him and handed him a wad of money through the window. Was this a drug deal or a simple money exchange? Either way, it was unsettling. We started driving again, but my heart was pounding. I was alone in a taxi with a man who had just received a large amount of money, no idea where I was, in the dark, with a dead cell phone. After another tense fifteen minutes, my phone showed a strip of green, and I immediately called the Casa. I put the receptionist on the phone with the driver to clarify the directions. It made me feel safer. Then I got in touch with one of my friends, who told me she'd greet me at the entrance when I arrived. Calming down a bit, I sat back and tried to relax. I'd spent so much energy and adrenaline just to get that far. I was exhausted when I finally arrived. My friend was there as promised, but I was just too tired to do anything but go to bed.

DURING

In the morning, I put on my whites and met my friends for breakfast of scrambled eggs and papaya. I told them the schlep story and they shared similar tales of hitting serious speed bumps on their way the first time they came to the Casa. We walked around the compound, a lovely place with open-air structures, mango and avocado trees, lilac and flowering plants. It reminded me of Mexico, tropical and pretty. Everyone wore white. About a thousand people from all over the world had come for clinic hours, and I picked up a contagious, communal positive energy from it. Some of the people were clearly ill, with shaved heads or in wheelchairs. Others seemed okay on the surface, but no one would make this journey if you weren't in dire need of something.

We went into a large, open room in the main building. On a small stage, JoG stood with a few members of his staff. He looked like an ordinary man with dark hair and a warm smile. The room filled with people speaking many languages. Each seeker was assigned a helper. Mine was a German woman who told me where to sit and meditate in the Current—the energy force that swirled around JoG. I sat for an hour and watched the transformation when the "entities" entered the body of JoG. His face changed. He seemed to be a different person. The entities were spirits of people who'd been doctors in their human lives, real people with names (alas, none were Marcus Welby). Each entity had a specialty, just like in a real hospital. But this was a spiritual hospital. Instead of sitting in a cold exam room in a paper gown, we sat in chairs or on the floor in the Current, in white cotton. Just like an actual hospital, though, there was a lot of waiting.

I know it sounds like a scam or a hoax. Along with a healthy dollop of skepticism, I brought with me a sense of curiosity and adventure. JoG charged nothing for the healing. You had to pay to get down there, and for your room and board in the Casa. But the price was low. If not for my complications with flights and extra travel expenses, it would have been the cheapest vacation I'd had in years. I figured I had nothing to lose. If the spiritual surgery worked, great. If not, I met some fabulous people and would come home with a great story.

In the late morning, the crowd lined up for twenty-second personal consultations with JoG. When it was my turn, my German helper introduced me to him and explained my situation. In Portuguese, he said, "Surgery."

He moved on to the next patient, and I was directed into a room with a few dozen other people to wait for him to perform a simultaneous psychic surgery on all of us. He finally came in, and said a few prayers in his native tongue. That, apparently, unleashed the entities to operate on us. He left and we continued to sit while our procedures were underway. Some people claimed they could feel snipping or cutting inside their bodies. I felt only mystified and confused. The entire process took all of five minutes. Then we were moved to a patio to get our instructions. One of the helpers asked, "Who had eye surgery?" Two of us raised our hand. She said, "Okay, now you go back to your Casa and you stay in your room for twenty-four hours. Do not read or look at a computer. People will bring you food."

My room in the Casa was very plain, a single room with a dresser and two twin beds. I worried about feeling bored in there for a whole day without any distractions. I got in bed and closed my eyes—and woke up sixteen hours later. I ate a bit of the basic vegetarian food, and then crashed again for hours.

In the morning, my German translator told me that my healing would continue over the next eight days, and then the entities would return to me, wherever I might be on the planet, to take out my "sutures." During the next eight days—four of them at the Casa—I could meditate, take long walks, talk to anyone, enjoy nature, sleep and eat, but I couldn't read or write. No books, phone, computer, nothing that might strain my eyes. Eight days without my communications? It'd be hell. I dictated a text to the helper to send to my kids, saying I'd be out of touch for a while, and felt a bit like crying.

I went on walks. I visited the glorious waterfall and let the sacred waters wash over me. I went to restaurants and ate pudding with bananas on top. I meditated and did my stretching exercises. I talked to strangers and my friends. All very nice and relaxing. Except being unplugged drove me mental. It was like withdrawal from a drug addiction. I couldn't stand it.

AFTER

On January 6 I flew home as planned. I had to stay off technology for another four days, but at least I'd be in the comfort of my condo. I taxied to the airport and got on my flight. Eight hours without TV wasn't as awful as I thought. I dozed and stared out the window. I almost asked the person next to me to read her book out loud. But it wasn't so onerous. In fact, I kind of enjoyed the mental challenge of keeping myself entertained within the confines of my own head.

I came to *like* being unplugged. Out of the habit of checking emails, reading blogs, and updating social media, I realized I didn't care about doing it. I loved the TV shows I watched, but realized I didn't need them to fill the hours. I could just as happily stare at the walls as if movies were playing upon them. It might've been the JoG effect I'd heard about, that after exposure to him, you felt blissful and calm. Taking a break from technology allowed me to go into myself, to really experience my thoughts and my body with no distractions. When you can't disappear into a book or a computer, you get a quick lesson on who you are and where your mind goes. Mine went to thoughts of gratitude and serenity, of quiet and peace. I'd never felt anything quite like that before, and it was a gift.

After filming for a couple of days in Dallas, I flew to New York for the network's upfronts, aka a big promotional presentation to media about the shows for the upcoming season. I mingled and met with press, but I didn't read or watch any screen—a challenge at an event about television. I had to avert my eyes constantly.

On the last night of my prescribed unplugging, I was in a hotel room in New York. I put on my whites before bed as instructed. Like the tooth fairy, the entities came in the night and removed my "sutures." In the morning, I had a big glass of water, as per protocol, and looked around.

My vision was the same, but I'd been told that it'd take some time for the effects to be fully realized.

WAY AFTER

It's been a year since my sutures came out. My vision is unchanged. But my outlook? Vastly improved.

The bulk of my spiritual gains happened before my arrival at the Casa, and way after my departure. Before, I'd had an international adventure and proved to myself the power of my determination. In the aftermath, I learned how to put aside the addiction of distraction. I gained awareness and redefined myself.

I was a doer. No visa? No problem. With the aid of new friends, I bulldozed my way into the jungle.

I was an adapter. No technology? I didn't need it after all. I could entertain myself perfectly well in my own mind. Distractions all seemed like wasted time compared to letting my brain ramble, allowing the big feels like love and gratitude with their wordless colors and shapes—what I imagined the "entities" recognized as pulsing auras—dazzle me for hours at a time. During those unplugged days, I was reminded of a quote from author Blaise Pascal: "All of humanity's problems stem from man's inability to sit quietly in a room alone."

I am a coper. No sight? I can cope with that, too. I might lose my eyes, but not sight of myself. There's nothing in my world that I'm afraid to look at, including the prospect of impending diminished sight. Perhaps my psychic eye surgery healed another part of me. I'm not afraid of anything anymore.

If we do adapt and cope, we can take on challenges. We adjust to change. We can learn not only to accept what we can't change, but to benefit from it in unexpected ways. As we get older, our bodies will betray us. Even the healthiest lifestyle and diet can't prevent deterioration. When the physical world fades, the spiritual becomes clearer. The mysteries of the universe—the kind of energy that JoG operates in—can't be seen by the sharpest, youngest eyes, but just because we can't see it doesn't mean it's not there. If we can be open to looking for the mysteries with our hearts and souls, we might catch a glimpse of something greater, more beautiful and divine than previously imagined. Even if I lost all my senses, I know I can look within for peace and serenity. I will ride the Current, the past and the future, of my adventurous life to wherever it takes me, no matter how far.

EXPAND YOUR WORLD

In the documentary *Joan Rivers: A Piece of Work*, there was a scene of Joan at seventy-five, preparing to host a Thanksgiving dinner. She talked about who was invited and the subject of friendships came up. "If something wonderful happens, there may be three people I'll call. Maybe. Fifteen years ago, there would have been six people I called," she said. "So many people are dying. They better eat fast tonight."

I can totally relate. Once upon a time, I had tons of friends. Where did they all go?

SOME FADED AWAY. I'm thinking of the people I went to school with, modeled with, lived near, met through work. Life threw us in close proximity to each other, but that didn't make us best friends forever. There were no dramatic blowups. I've never shoveled anyone out of my life. When this type of friendship ends, it's a slow fade. Calls aren't returned. Dates get canceled. Months, then years go by without contact, and the friend is relegated to "someone I used to know" status. I'd be happy to see someone I went to school with fifty years ago, like one of the bridesmaids at my wedding. We'd hug and say, "Wow! Good to see you. How have you been?" Catching up would give us both a warm glow—for an hour. And then we'd go our separate ways, content never to see or speak to each other again.

SOME FRIENDS DUMPED ME. When I became famous, a few of my friends expected me to start acting like a hoity-toity "star" with the air of superiority and a massive ego. But I wasn't different. I just had a camera on me. From the start, I felt their judgment as they backed slowly out of a friendship. I even understood it. You establish a friendship on a certain plane. Maybe one of you is prettier or richer or more successful but the dynamic is established, and you're comfortable with it or you wouldn't have become friends in the first place. A sudden shift in status throws the dynamic out of whack. Unless you can rebalance on a moving platform, the friendship is doomed. It doesn't mean you don't like the person. You just can't be friends anymore.

SOME SIDED WITH ED IN THE DIVORCE. While I was working on *Dallas*, Ed was going to dinners with our couple friends. If these friends were so easily swayed, they weren't worth having. Some were deathly embarrassed that my divorce played out in public, and couldn't bear to hang out with me. Back then, divorce was thought of as a contagious, disfiguring condition, especially for middle-aged women who were brought up to believe that their marriage defined them. As a single woman with money, I was seen as a threat, and was shunned. I didn't lose a single tear over these ex-BFs.

SOME CROSSED A LINE. I sympathize with child stars who lack the experience or maturity to sniff out the fakes, and are suckered into relationships with hangers-on. I can't say that I was fooled by phonies. I had their number from the start. And yet, there's an attractiveness to someone who seems fascinated by you and is always available. I got close to one or two hangers-on. When they crossed a line, though, the pseudo-friendships had to end. One woman, for example, made restaurant reservations in my name. When she showed up without me, she'd say, "Linda got called out of town at the last minute." I only learned about it when a maître d' at my favorite restaurant mentioned that this woman had come in with a bunch of her friends. I called her and said, "Not cool. You can't do that." I was furious, and she was so shamed and insulted, we never spoke again.

SOME WERE CASUALTIES OF CONTEXT. I'd befriended some of the moms at the kids' school. But when the kids graduated and moved on, so did the moms. Same story with some neighborhood pals. When they moved, the friendship was dislocated. I don't blame anyone for not keeping up those connections. We're all busy. Friendships are hard to maintain in the best of circumstances. When circumstances change and the common thread between you breaks, only the rare friendships last.

SOME WERE CRASHING DISAPPOINTMENTS. They seemed exciting at first, but then their petty dramas grew tedious. Or they presented as creative and visionary, which is a quality I gravitate toward in friendships and relationships. But then, despite having impressive minds, they were judgmental or critical, which is not to be tolerated, no matter how brilliant a person is. Or they lacked passion and couldn't understand how my passion for work was more important in my life than they were.

SOME WERE LOST TO ATTRITION. When I'm working, I don't have time to go to parties and lunch dates. After a while, I just get tired of hearing myself say that I'm too busy. The friends got tired of rejection, which made me feel awful. One applied the thumbscrews whenever I canceled plans. "Why haven't you called me back?" she asked. *Because you're a pain in the ass?* If you feel dread when you see a name pop up on your caller ID, that is not a friendship. It's a chore.

SOME DIED. Of all my lost friendships, the only ones I miss are the departed. Otherwise, I've been content to let connections go. I just don't see the point of maintaining a friendship that is more trouble than it's worth. At my age, friendship is all about fun. I used to judge closeness on whether I could cry in front of a person. Back then I was pretty bottled up. But now, if so moved, I can cry to just about anyone. It takes a special person to make me laugh from the gut, real endorphin-releasing belly howling. When I feel that explosion of joy, it's love. And if it's not love, why bother?

Friendship is very strange. You just pick a human you've met and you're like, "Yep, I like this one," and you just do stuff with them. At present, excluding colleagues, professional friends, acquaintances, and family members, I count only a few of what I call "heart friends," women I adore who adore me, comrades I trust implicitly and can count on at a moment's notice. My social circle has shrunk to the size of a dime. Who are my friends? I'll be vague about them, because they value their privacy. They are fabulous, strong, healthy, vibrant women. I'm the only actor and I'm considered an oddity. We met through mutual acquaintances, and had so much in common, we hit it off organically. They live all over the world. We stay connected via Skype, emails, phone calls, and elaborately planned vacations together. Our friendships are based on flexibility and understanding. If we can't return a call for a few days, there's no guilt trip or pressure. When we get together, we rush to hug and kiss, sit down, order food, laugh and start dishing all of our stories—and my pals always have great stories, usually about sex.

With so many people gone from my life—my sister, my parents, many beloved friends—and my social circle ever shrinking, I found myself asking, *Why am I still here? What am I supposed to be doing?*

I was fairly certain my grand purpose wasn't going to more parties and dinners. I knew I needed to serve and that growth came from giving, so when I was asked to be a United Nations Goodwill Ambassador to travel to developing countries, I jumped at the opportunity. Whenever you leave your safe environment and go into the world, you learn about yourself.

The purpose of going to Malawi was to feed the children. Our job was to distribute these forty-dollar bags of supergrain. Each bag would feed a child for a month, and the grain we provided was the only thing keeping them alive. We arrived at the village—it was just a dirt yard with makeshift shacks—and started handing the children their food, and their faces would just light up. One child led me by the hand to his mother and handed her his bag of food. She started cooking over an open fire, putting well water into pots and pans, pouring in the grain. We sat and talked with an interpreter as she stirred. All the women sat in a row, in front of their own little fires, and I sat with them on the ground. Despite having nothing, zero, the women were laughing and singing, so welcoming and charming to me. While we were cooking, the kids fashioned drums out of empty bottles and sticks, and started playing music for us. It's humbling, upsetting, and confusing to see poverty and joy at the same time. It was emotional and complicated, but I knew I was doing the right thing to be there and to feed these kids.

Children came with bowls to get the food we distributed. There was a rush at first and then a lull. The second wave of hungry kids had to wait for the first group to finish eating so they could use their bowls. A little boy asked me if I had a pen. I said, "I'm sorry, I don't." He told me that he needed a pen so he could go to school. No pen, no classes. I wish I had a hundred pens to give him.

I was in awe of these children for their courage and hope, and wanted to wrap each one of them in the protection of my arms. I would be the kind of friend that the children of the developing world needed most, someone who talked to them, about them, and for them. Buying one bag of grain can feed a child for a month. It costs next to nothing. Next time you have an obligatory lunch with a woman you wished you'd dumped years ago, cancel on the friend and donate the $40 to Feed the Children. You'll be so glad you did.

I have an expansive notion of what it means to be a friend, especially now as our social lives get smaller. It's not only about supporting those closest to you. It's being a friend of strangers who need your support a lot more. Because I've lost so many of the people I've loved doesn't mean my heart is smaller. I have just as much love to give as ever. Only now it radiates into the whole wide world.

HOW TO DATE AT ANY AGE

Younger people often ask me, "How do you meet men at your age? Do you even care about that anymore?"

I've got news for you, kids: When you're seventy-five, you are still going to be you. You'll still enjoy and seek out the company of an attractive man (or woman) who makes you feel sexy and feminine. And men will still seek out your company and think of you as a sexual being. Society is misleading to present seniors as asexual. We are who we've always been. You never stop caring about that. In fact, people my age might care about it even more because of our potential to enjoy it. We're no longer thinking about pregnancy, raising a young family, or money issues. We are more relaxed into fully appreciating the company of a partner, asking for what we want, and knowing our bodies well.

I meet men at parties and events and get fixed up through friends, the usual way. What attracts me to a man is his energy. I have a younger vibration, and I seem to be drawn to younger men. Not too much younger. A twenty-seven-year-old and I have too big a gap to bridge. Same thing with a ninety-year-old. If I respond to a man's energy, we're always in the same age ballpark. For that reason, I never ask a man how old he is. When I'm asked that question, I always feel taken aback. Why does he care? Why does it matter? If I choose to get intimate with someone I don't want them wondering how old I am.

After the chocolate and flowers and the "I love yous" must come appreciation. I want to feel valued for everything I am and everything I bring to the relationship. I'm a great lover of lingering eye contact. When you look someone in the eye, not over his shoulder, and you listen to him, you are fully engaged in conversation. You are living in the moment with that person. That's sexy. That's what I have to offer—the gift of undivided attention. In a real love connection, that gift is always returned.

We are vibrational beings. When we share our sexual vibration with someone else, there is a lovely energy exchange. It's pure and simple. We're not there to fix anything in each other, but simply to honor the time we are together. If that energy exchange is blocked by judgment, criticism, expectations, and demands, the reward of love and happiness isn't possible, and the relationship isn't worth continuing.

I've had many relationships since my divorce thirty-odd years ago. I adore men and have a strong drive to have fun. I also love my freedom. I fly all over the place for work and enjoy being able to pick up and go without negotiations or hurt feelings. If I want an apple for dinner at 6 p.m., or if I want chocolate at 9 p.m., there's no discussion about it. During the stretches when I'm between relationships, I grow through self-discovery. I honor that precious time and know that my next relationship will be deeper and more meaningful because of it.

You might be thinking, *Linda is scared of commitment because of her bad marriage. If she met the right man, she'd be happy to give up her freedom to be with him.*

We live in a couples-oriented society. (Don't be concerned if you are not a "couple." Your lessons are different than theirs.) I understand that a woman alone raises some questions and concerns. Does she hate men? Is she lonely?

I love men! They are not the enemy or the "bad guys." In general, women should give up expectations and accept them for who they are. But I also accept myself for who I am. I know that what matters most to me is having authority in my own life. In a relationship, you have to compromise and cede authority, at least somewhat. I also love falling in love. When I see a couple running through the grass holding hands and neither one is dragging the other, I feel romantic longing. I'm not averse to being in a passionate, long-term relationship. It just hasn't happened and I'm quite at peace with being by myself.

As far as loneliness is concerned, it's defined as the ache you feel when you desire the intimate company of others. When I need to be with people, I see a friend, or visit my kids, or spend the day with my grandsons. The truth is, my days are so full of things to do, I find myself craving more alone time. I've organized my life for maximum happiness, minimal aggravation, and that seems to have translated into my having exciting, if brief, relationships.

In all honesty, I do get lonely sometimes—for my dead cat. Dugie was the perfect bedmate. He snuggled against me, held my hand, and purred gently as we drifted off to sleep. What a good boy he was. I might get a new cat, but I'm quite content to stay an unmarried woman.

Crock-Pot Dinner for One (With Leftovers)

Since I'm cooking for myself and myself alone, here's one of my favorite Crock-Pot recipes that I make all the time.

Ingredients

1 medium zucchini, sliced thin

1 bunch fresh spinach, chopped

1 medium eggplant, sliced thin

1 clove of garlic, chopped

3 basil leaves chopped

1 package lasagna noodles (organic brown rice pasta)

1 package grated mozzarella cheese (goat, rice, almond, or tapioca cheese)

1 jar (25 oz.) tomato-basil marinara sauce, seasoned to taste

2 tbsp olive oil

Instructions

1. Warm up your slow cooker.

2. While chopping your ingredients, drop the olive oil in the pot.

3. Add half of the sliced onion and garlic.

4. Break uncooked lasagna noodle strips and cover the bottom of the pot with them.

5. Add a layer of sliced eggplant, red peppers, basil, and spinach.

6. Add sliced cheese.

7. Cover with half of the tomato sauce and seasoning.

8. Add another layer of lasagna noodle strips.

9. Add cheese, sliced zucchini, and the remaining chopped onion.

10. Cover with more sauce and seasoning.

11. Cook for about 2 or 2¹/₂ hours.

THE GRAY FOX

A fan letter:

HUSTLER

LARRY FLYNT
Chairman of the Board

June 21, 1983

Ms. Linda Gray
The William Morris Agency
151 El Camino Drive
Beverly Hills, California 90212

Attn: Mr. Fred Westheimer

Dear Ms. Gray:

HUSTLER MAGAZINE is looking for established female
celebrities to pose for our gala Tenth Anniversary
issue. The photo project can be completed in one
day, and we are willing to pay up to $1,000,000 for
the right person.

Should you have any interest, please contact me at
213-556-9200.

Sincerely,

LCF:mlr

2029 CENTURY PARK E.   LOS ANGELES, CALIFORNIA 90067   (213) 556-9200

245

He sent letters like this to many celebrities over the years. I didn't respond to Mr. Flynt's offer at the time, but I have a reply for him now.

Dear Mr. Flynt:

Thirty-two years ago, you offered me $1,000,000 to pose nude in Hustler *magazine. Forgive me for not answering at the time and for a while after. I've been busy. Things have slowed down a bit and I can now fit a photo shoot for your publication into my schedule. I assume the offer is still good? Of course, I'm far more experienced now so my rate has gone up. I look forward to working together!*

Sincerely,
Linda Gray

Think he'll take me up on it?

I don't look exactly the same as I did in 1983. But I'm not too shabby now, either. Except for a few gravity shifts, I haven't changed. I'm the same basic shape and volume I was then. I have the same come-hither bedroom eyes and the same saucy smile. My legs are just as long, and my chest is roughly the same cup size, although I'm not as perky as I used to be. My skin isn't as taut, and it's got some marks on it, but it is still skin, which Mr. Flynt trades in.

We all want that dewy wrinkle-free skin, but as we notice the changes, we also notice our growth as human beings. Not everyone is as attuned to that as they could be. Nora Ephron wrote a whole book about it—*I Feel Bad About My Neck*—and described how upsetting it was for her to look in the mirror as she aged. For such an accomplished, brilliant woman to be that devastated about natural body changes surprised me. If you're driven to depression over a few wrinkles, your self-loathing runs deeper than the surface of your skin. A word to anyone who gets that depressed about a wrinkle: Getting old is inevitable. Aging is optional.

Perhaps women who cry about their necks, spots, crepey upper arms are afraid their husbands won't love them unless their boobs were perky like a teenager's. If that were true, the problem isn't saggy tits. Perhaps they equate a saggy behind with imminent death. In my opinion, a soft tush is just a soft tush. We're all doing the best we can with what we were given. We can choose to exercise and eat right. We can choose not to smoke and keep the drinking to a minimum. Or not. It's your choice. Having survived this long and lived a full life, you've earned the right to stop fretting about looking your age. Relax into looser skin.

We spend an inordinate amount of time, energy, and money on keeping our outsides "young," without paying much attention at all to our insides. If our innards are aging rapidly, it doesn't matter what you look like. I've already given you my speeches about organic greens and cutting out sweets, meats, and wheat, so I won't repeat myself. But we do need to have a serious discussion about stress. I'm referring to the acute "fight or flight" sudden flare of stress you get on the highway, but also the chronic stress of life, the demands, rushing, responsibilities, and worries that accumulate in your body over time. Along with sapping energy, vitality, and happiness, stress takes a huge toll on our health, especially as we age.

STRESS ACCELERATES THE BIOLOGICAL AGING. Think of how New England winters affect a house. Stress is like a storm beating down our bodies. Over time, we're worse than weathered. Withered.

STRESS WEAKENS OUR IMMUNE SYSTEM, which isn't as good as it used to be anyway. Under stress, we're more susceptible to colds, flu, pneumonia, and a host of other sicknesses. Wounds take forever to heal. Broken bones don't stitch back together.

STRESS INCREASES INFLAMMATION. Internal inflammation doesn't sound like such a big deal. So what if your innards are a little red and puffy?

Chronic inflammation leads to all kinds of horrid age-related diseases, such as atherosclerosis, osteoporosis, arthritis, Type 2 diabetes, and cancers.

STRESS CAUSES DECAY. Oxidation stress is what happens when food and environmental toxins build up in your kidneys, colon, liver, heart, blood vessels, and other organs, and slowly turn them to rust. You can avoid some toxins by eating organic (there I go again) and being a royal pain in the ass at restaurants, asking how food is prepared, if it's cooked on scratched Teflon, which oils are used. You do not want to eat out with me if you can't stand a high-maintenance eater. I ask about everything, from ingredients to cooking vessels. If you can cut out half the toxins in your diet, great. The environmental toxins in the air and water, the chemicals in our furniture, cleaning supplies, etc., are unavoidable. Cleanse with some of the methods I've mentioned before: dry brushing, jumping on a rebounder, yoga, salt baths, infrared saunas, massage. Move those toxins through your lymphatic system and out through your pores and bowel.

STRESS IMBALANCES HORMONES. I was introduced to Michael Galitzer, M.D., through friends and he's given me an education about all my glands and how to keep my hormones in balance. His book *Outstanding Health* is a must read. We have all these glands pumping out hormones, and stress is the monkey wrench in the works. It's vital for women to learn about their adrenal gland—What is it? What's it do? Is it functioning properly? There are telltale signs. When my adrenals are whipped (meaning, over-producing cortisol), I crave coffee like a maniac. That's when I know I'm out of balance. What about other glands—the thyroid and pituitary? Are they all functional? If one isn't working well, they're all shot. Our hormones are all interconnected and way too complicated to explain here. But Dr. Galitzer does a fine job in his book. Or you can research it online. It's a perfect time to take control and become an expert on who we are; what makes us tick; what makes us sick.

STRESS MAKES YOU FORGETFUL. Even minor stressors, like driving in a strange city, can make perfectly healthy adults forget where their hotel is located. Why? When you're stressed out, cortisol floods the hippocampus and amygdala, the parts of the brain that govern long- and short-term memory. Chronic cortisol flooding damages brain cells. In our senior years, all of our systems slow down, including the one that lets cortisol exit our brains after a stressful episode. It gets stuck in there, making us stress and forget for longer periods, further dismantling cells. We laugh about having "senior moments." Not quite so funny when you know what's causing them: decades of slow and steady brain damage. Women are three times as likely as men to experience the chipping away of our cognition, probably because we've been the longtime official family worriers. I hesitate to mention the link between stress, high blood pressure, and dementia. One plus one equals . . . um, what were we talking about again?

The cumulative effects of a lifetime of stress hit us at the same time we go through life's most stressful situations. Losing loved ones. Moving. (Even if you *want* to downsize, it's still stressful to pack up and give away a lifetime of accumulation, and go live in an unfamiliar, new place.) Getting a frightening diagnosis. Watching your bank account dwindle, even if you've planned well for retirement. It's the ultimate double whammy. I'm sorry to say, no amount of yoga can undo the damage that stress has already done to your body. You *can* use de-stressing techniques to prevent further insult, add years to your life, and relaxation to your years.

EXERCISE. It'd been proven to lower cortisol rates, in particular, in women over sixty. It doesn't have to be much. A walk every day. A gentle stretch yoga class. Paddling around the pool. In fact, you should take it easy. If you go hard and take a manic spin class or jog five miles, you will cause a stress response in your body and weaken the muscles and immune system you're trying to strengthen. Just get moving. A half an hour a day will do wonders.

SOCIALIZING. Best-case scenario: Go on your daily walk with a friend. Not only will socializing with friends and family—or a stranger at the supermarket, someone you sit next to on a plane, another volunteer at the soup kitchen—stem the flow of stress hormones, it keeps your mind sharp.

PETS. Get a pet! Studies have shown that an animal reduces stress and alleviates grief. Dogs force you to go on walks and bend down to pick up poop (see above re: exercise).

PUZZLES AND MEMORY GAMES. Is it normal to forget why you entered a room the second you got there, or people's names? Deterioration is a natural process, but we can slow it down and keep our brains functioning at optimum capacity with challenging activity. For *Cinderella*, I signed on to do two shows a day, every day, for six weeks, an intimidating and grueling schedule. But that was easy compared to memorizing twenty pages of rhyming couplets. During rehearsals, my brain cells felt like two sticks rubbing together, trying to make a spark. I'd memorize a page, move on to to the next, and then completely forget what I'd just nailed down. After a week, thank God, my synapses finally caught fire. My memory stretched in unaccustomed ways to get the pacing and rhythm. I could almost feel the new pathways burning through my grey matter. Much to my amazement—and profound relief—I'd accomplished something completely new and locked in those rhymes. My brain wasn't a dried-up sponge! Old sparky still had some juice.

Experts would say that the reason my brain could meet the challenge of that daunting task was because I've been memorizing scripts and have been an avid reader for my whole life. Puzzles, music, and memorization stimulate the brain and keep the synapses warm. Crossword puzzles have been proven to help prevent Alzheimer's. Any puzzle helps. Sudoku. Tetris. Judging by Facebook, Candy Crush is very popular. It's worth a try.

OPTIMISM. Pessimist readers may scoff, believing that you're born to be a "half-full" or "half-empty" person. Not true. You can choose to have a positive attitude. We have prejudices about ourselves, just as we might about others. One is the belief that we are who we are and can't alter our mind-set. I know it's possible, because I did it myself. It's a matter of flipping the switch in your mind. For some, it might be flipping from "no" to "yes." I flipped in the opposite direction. I was a classic doormat "yes woman." When I learned to stand up for myself and say "no," my outlook changed.

In 1978, an artist friend of Larry and Maj Hagman's was having an art exhibit in Dallas in a small gallery in Oak Lawn. We'd just started filming the first season, and I guess Larry picked up on my "yes woman" tendencies. At the art show, Larry and his friend dragged me over to see one piece that they said I had to buy. It was large, 44 x 56 inches of overlapping one-inch squares with the word "no" on each. The painting was named "No, No, No . . . A Thousand Times No." I bought it and it still hangs in my hallway. I walk by it every day to remind myself that it's essential to say no. Among the few possessions I plan to take with me to my grave, this is one of them.

Playing games, relaxing, and chilling with kids and cats will make us live longer, happier, and better. While saying "no" to stress is important, it's just as important to say "yes" to fun, adventure, new challenges, and opportunities. Which is why I'm saying a resounding "yes" to *Hustler: Gray Foxes Edition.* I'm stating for the record that if you write a check for twenty-five million dollars to Enid Borden at the National Foundation to End Senior Hunger and twenty-five million dollars to me, I will pose for your magazine. Let's get this thing going. Neither one of us is getting any prettier, Mr. Flynt. I'm waiting by the phone. Call me!

SHINE, BABY, SHINE

Last fall, I was invited to give the keynote address at the 2014 Ultimate Women's Expo in Dallas. What is the Ultimate Women's Expo? Does it involve female cage wrestling? No. It's like Comic Con soaking in an ocean of estrogen. Lots of shopping, massages, makeovers, style consultations, and panel discussions on money, relationships, beauty, and nutrition. My talk was scheduled for midday. The attendants would face a tough choice: lunch, a free eyebrow wax, a jewelry design workshop, or listening to me drop some nuggets of wisdom about life. I'd been alive for three-quarters of a century. Surely, I had something powerful and inspiring to offer them.

I considered opening with the line, "You've got only one life. So enjoy it now because, someday you're going to die," but it didn't seem like the right tone. I might, however, embroider that line on a pillow.

For a week, I scribbled notes and then threw them out. Acting was easy; motivational speech writing was *hard*. What could I offer women that would resonate with them—and with me? I could just trot out the old *Dallas* stories, but I'd already hashed and rehashed that material so many times already.

I kept coming back to one word. Shine. When Larry Hagman was nearing the end of his life, he got a gig representing a solar power company. He wore a button on his lapel that said, "Shine Baby Shine," and used the phrase for "hello," "good-bye," and "peace." The Larry Hagman version of "shalom."

Shine. In one word, it radiated the ultimate truth. My speech and my message would be about how each of us can find our unique spark to shine, baby, shine.

Marianne Williamson put it perfectly when she wrote in *A Course in Miracles*, "We are all meant to shine, as children do. We were born to make manifest the glory of God that is within us. It's not just in some of us; it's in everyone. And as we let our own light shine, we unconsciously give other people permission to do the same. As we are liberated from our own fear, our presence automatically liberates others."

Yes, we're all born with a spark of magnificence. But life gets so busy and we have so many demands put on us by others, our spark gets buried deeper than a dog buries a bone. We not only forget it's there. We forget how to find it. By my age, digging up that spark and brushing it off is the most precious gift we can give ourselves. If we believe we are magic, we become whole. We feel complete. The thing that we might've felt was missing all along is found. It's inside each one of us. If we find our brilliance, we are emboldened to share it with the world.

When the spark dims, relationships fail. Careers get stuck. Our worst fears and insecurities expand and confidence dwindles. Our lives don't unfold the way they should. We work as hard as we can and still feel dissatisfied and unfulfilled. I've been there many times. Those were the dark days.

I didn't really come into my own until sixty, when I made a solid decision to choose to be happy. I resolved to make the life I wanted.

Until then, I thought my happiness had to be linked to other people. But then I realized happiness had to start with me. I had to give myself permission to be first, to love and nurture myself first, and to be honest about my strengths and my weaknesses. Once I did the hard emotional work of figuring out exactly who I was, I could give of myself, love more deeply, and let my essential nature, with all my flaws, shine. The brightest times in my life have been when I didn't hide my light. I want to shine continuously. I won't settle for less. No one should.

So this is pretty much what I decided to share with the ladies at the Expo. They were going to look at me like I'd was completely New Age California woowoo. But one excellent aspect about being my age? I didn't care what they thought of me. I wanted to do a good job for myself and to speak my truth. If they couldn't handle my truth, that was their loss.

I opened up by asking the audience, "How do you define yourself?" Blank looks from the ladies.

"If you immediately thought 'wife,' or 'mother,' or your job title, think again," I said. "You're not so-and-so's wife, or daughter, or mother. Who are you apart from the roles you play for other people?"

The ladies now looked visibly anxious. They glanced from side to side at each other and shuffled in their seats. A woman around my age in the front row turned to her friend and said, "I thought she was going to tell funny stories about Larry Hagman and Patrick Duffy."

I let the question hang there for a minute and just stared at the women I could see. The tension in the room was taut. I knew I must have hit a nerve.

"What do you care about?" I asked. "Where do you fit into the grand scheme?" After a pause, I asked, "What the hell *is* the grand scheme anyway?" The women laughed, but I could tell they were still confused. Then I explained the concept of how we're all born to be brilliant, but we lose sight of our unique spark under piles and piles of distractions, addictions, insecurities, obligations, and the busy work of life.

"You're not who you used to be, or who you hope to be, or who other people expect you to be," I told the ladies. "You have to peel a lot of layers to figure out who you really are and what matters to you. When you know yourself and your true purpose, you are at peace. Everything else is bullshit."

I didn't say it in exactly those words, but the ladies got my point.

"We have to say 'yes' to life and let go of the anxiety, perfectionism, and resistance that holds us back," I said. "We have to play more and find work that is inspiring, something we feel enthusiastic about. We must shed what doesn't matter and embrace what does, by living with compassion, love, and charity. We have to learn from every step of our journey and always seek out the spirit of adventure."

Next, I opened the floor for audience members to discuss the ongoing process of self-discovery, the continual search for the spark. How to go about uncovering it? I suggested the things I've been talking about for the last two hundred pages: Be grateful for every blessing. Meditate. Stop struggling in relationships and worrying about your wrinkles. Share. Let go of prejudices, especially the ones we have about ourselves. Shed possessions, addictions, grudges, and anger. Exercise your body and your mind. Be generous. See the world. Shrug off the small stuff and the big stuff. Treasure the friends you have and honor the memory of those you've lost. Don't live in fear of death; be full of joy you're not dead yet. Every morning your feet hit the floor, say, "Thank you."

My speech turned into a group therapy session. Afterward, women came up to me to thank me and dig deeper. I was struck by the universality of womankind. These women had the same complaints as others I'd met all over the world, and we all want the same things: That our lives run smoothly, that the bills get paid, that our loved ones are healthy, and our relationships are strong and fulfilling. But we take on too much. We feel compelled to be all things to all people instead of prioritizing ourselves. We can't help others unless we help ourselves first.

I'll share one more list with you. It's the To Do list to end all To Do lists. It's everything you need to enjoy life. Take the Time to: Love and Give, and Shine, Goddess, Shine!

That pretty much says it all. I might have to retire my yellow legal pads now.

ACKNOWLEDGMENTS

Writing a book is daunting—and that is an understatement. Since this is my first book, I was educated each and every step of the way by such outstanding people. I had met Jan Miller in the '80s while we were filming the original *Dallas*. We remained friends through all those years and when we met for dinner one evening two years ago, while we were filming the new *Dallas*, I told her that someone had approached me to write a book and I wanted to get her advice! By then she had become the top literary agent for hundreds of *New York Times* bestsellers. She sat back in her chair and looked at me with a look that could rival Sue Ellen's, and said, "You can't do a book without me!" I was thrilled and felt like I would be nurtured through this new adventure with her at the helm. She kept saying to me, "What's the reveal?" I will be forever grateful to her for her loving guidance.

She turned me over to Nena Madonia, whom I wanted to adopt immediately! She is smart, savvy, has the energy of a hummingbird, and is passionate about making a book the best it can be.

Whatever would I do without Jeffrey Lane in my life? Jeffrey is my publicist and we have worked together for twenty-five years! We speak every morning like clockwork. He has been a constant support through both the good and bad times. Bless you and thank you for looking after me so beautifully Jeffrey.

When I first met Judith Regan in New York, I was drawn to her like a long lost friend. Five minutes into our meeting I felt as if I had known her forever. We were two grown-ups who could speak of subjects that younger people couldn't relate to. When she agreed to publish my book I was thrilled. Her last words to me were, "Be bold."

Valerie Frankel . . . writer extraordinaire. Because of our wacky *Dallas* shooting schedule, I would send Val my scribbles on yellow legal tablets and she would miraculously make sense of them. She came to my home to meet me face-to-face and then we would do Skype sessions from then on, especially when I was working in London. Thanks will never be enough to tell you how grateful I am for your continued support.

Alexis Gargagliano is an angel. We met at Judith's office in New York as she sat with several Post-it notes sticking out of the manuscript. Corrections, questions, deletions, and all the things a very focused editor does, Alexis does well. Terror turned into calm as she started her process with me. She is clear, calm, and caring! Everything I could wish for in an editor. Thank you, dear Alexis.

There are so many talented and creative people at Regan Arts that have touched this project: Kurt Andrews, George Bick, Tracy Brickman, Lynne Ciccaglione, Richard Ljoenes, and Nancy Singer. You all are so appreciated for your attention to every single detail of the book. You have made sure that as I handed over my baby it would be looked after and nurtured through the entire process.

I bless all the people I have mentioned in the book as they were the reasons my adventures developed. And the men who showed up in my life for both of us to learn lessons of how to be in relationship. That's what this entire process has been for me. An adventure that dragged me kicking and screaming into crevices of my mind that I thought I had forgotten. I hope that Jan Miller got the reveal she was looking for and that I was bold enough for Judith Regan.

Gratitude to all of you for making my 75th birthday so memorable.

IMAGE CREDITS